Service Living

Service Living
Building Community through Public Parks and Recreation

by

Doug Wellman, Dan Dustin,
Karla Henderson, and Roger Moore

Venture Publishing, Inc.
•••
State College, Pennsylvania

Production Manager: Richard Yocum
Manuscript Editing: Richard Yocum and George Lauer
Cover Design: Liza Cruze and George Lauer
Library of Congress Catalogue Card Number: 2008934811
ISBN-10: 1-892132-82-6
ISBN-13: 978-1-892132-82-6

For
a human
character to reveal
truly exceptional qualities,
one must have the good fortune
to be able to observe its
performance over many years.
If this performance is devoid of all egoism,
if its guiding motive is unparalleled generosity,
if it is absolutely certain that there
is no thought of recompense and that,
in addition, it
has left its
visible mark
upon the earth,
then there can be no mistake.

—Jean Giono, *The Man Who Planted Trees*

Dedication

To the memory of
Frederick Law Olmsted, Jane Addams, Benton MacKaye,
and Marjory Stoneman Douglas
who, by their example, teach and inspire us to live a life of service

Acknowledgments

We are indebted to Venture Publishing, Inc. of State College, Pennsylvania for making this book possible. From concept to completion the Venture staff has supported us. We would also like to thank the many people whose ideas have informed our thinking along the way, and our colleagues, friends, and families who sustain us. We extend our appreciation as well to Barbara Brock, Adrienne Cachelin, Patti Clayton, Liza Cruze, Tom Goodale, Kirk Nichols, Jeff Rose, Keri Schwab, and Janet Wellman for their critical review of various sections of the manuscript. Finally, we would like to thank our students who motivate us to contemplate and write about the future. We trust this book will be a welcome companion for anyone who is dedicated to making the world a better place through service living.

Service living honors that part of each of us that is connected to the larger community of life. It is lifelong action that contributes to the health and well-being of all living things.

Table of Contents

Preface

At a time in American history when there are more than 300 million citizens dotting the landscape, it is all too easy for us to think it impossible for one person to make much of a difference. Our inclination is to leave the business of a democracy to the select few—the politicians and their appointees. We retreat into the comfort and safety of our private lives and forsake public service. We leave "looking after the public good" to someone else.

This book challenges us to reconsider what it means to be responsible citizens in a participatory democracy. It asks us to see ourselves not only as individuals, but as part of a much larger unfolding story—the growth and development of a nation. It suggests that we have both the opportunity and the obligation to become engaged in public life, and that such engagement defines a life worth living. The book suggests further that self-fulfillment, if it is to come our way, will be a byproduct of that engagement.

We make our case by telling the stories of four individuals who made remarkable contributions to our nation's history: Frederick Law Olmsted, Jane Addams, Benton MacKaye, and Marjory Stoneman Douglas. In many respects, these four people were ordinary citizens going about their business, experiencing life's ups and downs, suffering through self-doubt, insecurity, and anxiety, just like the rest of us. But they also transcended their individualism to do something extraordinary to promote the public good. They were living proof that each one of us can make a positive difference in this world if only we would try. How they did it, and how we can do it as well, is through service living.

I
Why Service Living?

In *Reflections from the North Country,* Sigurd Olson suggests that the greatest achievement in our flight to the moon is "a picture of the earth, a living blue-green planet whirling in the dark endless void of space, and the realization that this is home."[1] From space we see no political, cultural, or social boundaries. From space we see no ideological schisms. From space we see only one ecological reality within which we must learn to live our lives. This ecological reality is marked not by separateness and autonomy, but by interconnectedness and interdependence. It consists of a web of relationships. Ecology's message to us is crystal clear. We live on this planet together and we should conduct ourselves in ways that reflect a conscious appreciation of the condition of the rest of the world.

As you read this book, we ask that you keep this image of a "living blue-green planet whirling in the dark endless void of space" in your mind's eye. It is an image that colors almost everything we have to say. As you will see in this introductory chapter, if "I" is the domain of psychology, and "we" is the domain of sociology, then "I" and "we" together is the domain of ecology.[2] Indeed, what we call "service living" is rooted in this ecological worldview. It challenges the conventional wisdom of seeing ourselves as separate and autonomous beings. Service living stems from seeing ourselves as interdependent parts of a larger organic whole.

Our overarching purpose in writing the book is to call each of us to public service based on the understanding that we are part of a much larger community of life, a community that is in dire need of the gift of service we each have to offer. Moreover, we write to remind ourselves that it is the self in service to others that gives life its meaning. Service living is distinguished by lifelong action that contributes to the health and well-being of all living things. It operationalizes the ecological worldview because through it we attend to the connections between our own lives, other lives, and the systems and relationships that comprise the whole.[3]

When we say "public service," we do not mean that we have to drop everything and run for public office. What we mean is that each of us should acknowledge and seek to strengthen that part of ourselves that is attached to something larger—family, community, nation, and world. To live a self-absorbed life does not lead to fulfillment. It leads to self-aggrandizement. It does not do justice to the part of our lives that is inextricably bound up with the welfare of others. We are trying to reach that part in this book. That part of each of us is potentially ennobling.

We understand that we are not all equally positioned to give of ourselves. Those among us who are struggling to make ends meet, or who are working more than one job to get by, are disadvantaged. Providing the basic essentials of life drains much of the time and energy that we might otherwise devote to working on behalf of the public good. Nonetheless, we believe each of us has the ability to contribute something. Little things matter and the cumulative effects of our individual actions often result in major positive changes. Our personal challenge, therefore, is to do what we can.

To illustrate the possibilities, we devote the heart of our book to telling you the stories of four remarkable people who exemplified service living: Frederick Law Olmsted, Jane Addams, Benton MacKaye, and Marjory Stoneman Douglas. Their stories are representations of the larger story of our nation's growth and development. In the final chapter, we will discuss the lessons learned from the four biographies that we can apply to our own lives. We will also discuss what makes living in a democracy fertile ground for service living, and we will conclude by calling each of us to a life of service that is meaningful, sustainable, and fulfilling.

To set the stage for what follows, we must first take a closer look at how we Americans came to see ourselves not as interconnected and interdependent beings but as separate and autonomous beings, and why that perspective does not bode well for the future. To accomplish this, we have to look back on a United States of America that developed a penchant for self-reliance and individualism long before humankind first set foot on the moon.

America's Faith in Self-Reliance

The great American western film *High Noon* begins on a happy note. The marshal who has brought law and order to the town is one day from retirement, and he and the woman he is about to marry are enjoying the company and congratulations of the townsfolk. After a simple civil ceremony in his office, the marshal and his new bride are preparing to depart for their new life when news breaks that a vicious killer he sent to prison years ago has been released. Three of the killer's accomplices ride through town and head to the train station, where their boss will arrive at 12 o'clock noon. Their clear intent is to gun down the man who sent him to jail. Implored by his new bride and his friends to leave town, the marshal refuses, arguing that it's his duty to continue protecting the public until the new marshal arrives the next day. As the clock mercilessly advances toward high noon, one after another of the marshal's supporters find excuses for not standing with him. He is left to face the killers alone.

High Noon is a Hollywood movie, and the marshal prevails through courage and guile—and surprising help from his pacifist wife. One by one, the killers are dispatched. As the movie ends, the townsfolk slowly emerge from hiding to gather around the marshal and his bride. Without a word, he communicates his disgust at their cowardice by throwing his badge to the ground and riding out of town.

High Noon has a compelling narrative, an outstanding cast, memorable music, and brilliant cinematography, but those elements alone do not account for its high standing in American film history. The movie is among our favorites because it engages one of the quintessential elements of our American character, a reverence for self-reliance and a deep, almost unconscious belief that success or failure depends, in the final analysis, on individual action. At crunch time, *High Noon* tells us, we really are on our own.

We take issue with the central premise of *High Noon*. We suggest that America's unquestioned faith in self-reliance must be balanced with widespread civic engagement if our democracy is to prosper. Indeed, our motivation for writing the book stems, in part, from our collective disappointment with the general retreat from public life exhibited by so many Americans in so many ways over so many years. As Robert Putnam chronicled in *Bowling Alone: the Collapse and Revival of American Community*,[4] this fundamental withdrawal from public life challenges the foundation of our democracy. It deprives us of the social capital that is required for our nation's growth and development. We all need to pitch in and work cooperatively to build a future of peace, well-being, and justice for all. But how is it, you might wonder, that we came to withdraw from one another in the first place?

Radical Individualism's Threat to Democracy

In their 1985 book *Habits of the Heart: Individualism and Commitment in American Life*,[5] Robert Bellah, Richard Madsen, William Sullivan, Ann Swindler, and Steven Tipton explore American culture and the future prospects for our democracy. The book has enjoyed best-seller status and it seems to have touched a nerve with many Americans. *Habits of the Heart* is a searching exploration of the fundamental American values of liberty and individualism and the unfortunate consequences of pushing these values too far.

Bellah and his co-authors derived the title for their book from the work of the 19th century French social philosopher Alexis de Tocqueville. In *Democracy in America*,[6] Tocqueville reported on his travels and observations of American society in the 1830s as he sought to gauge the prospects for success in our experiment with democracy. He interviewed many Americans and described their customary, unquestioned ways of thinking. He called those widely shared ways of thinking "habits of the heart." They provided Tocqueville with keys to understanding what was distinct about the American character, and they guided his assessment of American democracy's chances for long-term success.

Tocqueville warned that American individualism might eventually isolate and insulate citizens from one another and thereby undermine the conditions for freedom.[7] But he also identified some features of American life—the strength of family ties, the ethical teachings of our religious traditions, and our participation in local politics—that would work to create citizens who could sustain a connection to a wider political community and support the maintenance of free institutions.

Habits of the Heart focuses on American individualism as its central theme. Writing one and one-half centuries after Tocqueville, its authors worry that family life, religious traditions, and local political participation—the traits that Tocqueville thought would moderate against radical individualism—have fallen into disrepair while individualism has grown out of control. They put it bluntly:

> We are concerned that this individualism may have grown cancerous—that it may be destroying those social integuments that Tocqueville saw as moderating its more destructive potentialities, that it may be threatening the survival of freedom itself.[8]

In 1996, ten years after publication of the original edition of *Habits of the Heart,* Bellah and his colleagues published a second edition. In an extended new introduction, they found their worries about the dominance of "radical individualism" over "associational involvement" had only grown deeper over the years:

> We are divided, we are told, by race, by culture, by creed, by differing views of the national identity. But we are united, as it turns out, in at least one core belief, even across lines of color, religion, region, and occupation: the belief that economic success or misfortune is the individual's responsibility, and his or hers alone.[9]

American allegiance to individualism and self-reliance can be traced back to colonial times and the New World's settlers who were fleeing oppression in Europe. Fed up with being denied their individual rights by the tyranny of the wealthy and aristocratic, they were unquestionably seeking equality of opportunity in their new homeland. Individualism became one of the principal manifestations of that quest. Two hundred years after the Revolutionary War, *Habits of the Heart*'s authors conclude that individualism is now so deeply engrained in the American character that we take it for granted. It is part of our identity. As a result, and unlike most other industrialized nations, we leave problems of personal, social, and environmental welfare almost entirely to the individual to resolve. We see almost everything as a matter of individual responsibility.

Individualism certainly has provided the foundation for capitalism to prosper in the United States. We continue to believe in the promise of Adam Smith's "invisible hand," the idea that an individual who looks out for his or her own best interest will be led "by an invisible hand" to promote the public interest.[10] However, while capitalism has brought great wealth and power to our nation, there is growing unease throughout the country that things may not be going exactly as planned. *Habits of the Heart* describes Americans' uneasiness about the soundness of our society and its prospects for the future. Some people doubt the ability of institutions, elected officials, neighbors, or even themselves to live up to the expectations for their lives. Many worry about crime, moral decline, and the deepening divides of income and opportunity. Anxiety is commonplace.

Economic and Social Manifestations of Radical Individualism

Changes in the national economy explain many of the problems in contemporary American life as well as the widespread anxiety about the future. Jobs that were once secure have been lost to innovations in manufacturing, global trade, and market forces far beyond the understanding and control of average people. Government programs for the poor and middle class have been reduced, discontinued, and threatened, and the gulf between the haves and have-nots has widened dramatically in recent years. American workers have not been able to capture the benefits of their nation's rising productivity. In the 20 years from 1973 to 1993, "real per capita gross domestic product went up 29 percent … (but) …80 percent of workers either lost ground or barely held their own."[11] Economist Lester Thurow calls this situation unprecedented: "Never before have a majority of American workers suffered real wage reductions while the per capita domestic product was advancing."[12] The authors of *Habits of the Heart* note that by comparison, other high-tech economies in Europe and Asia have found ways to share the wealth that has arisen from improved productivity.[13]

Columnist Ellen Goodman asks how these unfortunate and destructive changes have come about. Echoing *Habits of the Heart,* she points the finger at radical individualism:

> Hacker (a political scientist) blames the conservative's 'personal responsibility crusade.' 'Political leaders told us that we need to take ownership of our economic future and personal responsibility for our lives.'

This tapped into the primal American belief in independence, individualism, bootstraps. It tapped out the other modulating American belief that we should insure each other from the hazards of illness, old age, and unemployment…we're told, 'You can do it,' without being told, 'We can help.'

…we have yet to develop a narrative, a story for the 21st century with all its globalism and change that counters the simplistic, powerful notion of individual responsibility.[14]

Habits of the Heart's authors contend that American individualism has been sustainable over time only because it has been supported and checked by moral understandings grounded in religious and civic traditions. The Bible, which served as a guide to ethical behavior for the nation's founders, teaches concern for the intrinsic value of individuals because of their relationship to the transcendent. The civic traditions of the founders also saw American democracy as a project of common moral purpose that holds citizens responsible for the common good. These ideas remind us that being an individual— being one's own person—does not mean escaping ties to others. Real freedom lies not in rejecting our social nature but in fulfilling it by acknowledging a common responsibility to a wider fellowship of life. This insight is one of ecology's great gifts to us.

Bellah and his colleagues suggest that the consequences of radical individualism are more evident than ever as shown by declines in civic engagement and community involvement. The rich, with their ties to local communities weakened by frequent corporate moves, retreat into gated enclaves and secure offices. Many of them feel less obliged than their privileged forbears to give back to the larger community through leadership of civic organizations and projects. At the other end of the spectrum, poverty forces the poor to focus exclusively on life's most basic necessities, which blocks their participation in civic life. People in the middle—Robert Reich calls them the "anxious class"—are buffeted by stagnant or declining wages, and they are suspicious not only of government but also of organizations of any kind.[15] To the extent any of the social classes are involved in political life, it tends to take the form of monetary contributions that do not deepen civic culture or social capital.

Self-Interest and the Common Good

How have we reached this point in American history when government action for the common good is disparaged and people would rather sit home and watch TV than participate in making their communities better? The search for balance between emphasizing the good of the individual and the good of the community is probably as old as human history. It has certainly been a long featured dynamic of our society. The laissez-faire capitalism of the latter 19th century, for example, created amazing wealth, but it also promoted economic and social disparities that threatened continuation of American democracy. Industrialists like J. P. Morgan and Cornelius Vanderbilt displayed their fabulous riches through conspicuous consumption,[16] while the working poor, including many children, toiled in dangerous conditions for low wages. The large influx of European immigrants created a large labor pool that kept wages low and undercut worker resistance to oppression—they knew if they complained they could and would quickly be replaced by someone even hungrier.

Drawing on Charles Darwin's *On the Origin of Species,* British philosopher Herbert Spencer provided the rationalization that justified these exploitative conditions. Spencer argued that extremes of wealth and poverty were acceptable—in fact, necessary—for human progress. Any action by government to protect the worker or force the well-to-do to share their wealth was wrong since it would interfere with the laws of nature—the "survival of the fittest."

Responding to the excesses of the Gilded Age, the Progressive movement of the early 20th century built the case for an active government that would pursue scientifically based planning and management in pursuit of the common good. But what is the common good? Political scientists today are uncomfortable with the term because it defies clear definition. Since the United States' population is both large and extremely diverse, and since any given public action will be seen as favoring some groups over others, it seems we can never define the public good or the public interest in a manner that will satisfy everyone.

James Madison and other founding fathers had far less difficulty talking about the common good. Living in a much less populated and diverse America, they believed the democratic government they created "…could survive only if animated by a spirit of virtue and concern for the common good."[17] In *The Federalist Papers,* Madison noted that "…the public good, the real welfare of the great body of the people, is the supreme object to be pursued." Following the French philosopher Montesquieu, the founders believed that the key to a self-sustaining republic was civic virtue and that "…the virtuous citizen was one who understood that personal welfare is dependent on the general welfare."

The authors of *Habits of the Heart* identify a number of competing visions of the public good in contemporary life. As they explain, these visions represent "…different proposals for how best to make sense of that basic tension between individualism and the common good as this tension has grown in the industrial age."[18] Two key visions are "Welfare Liberalism" and "Neocapitalism." Welfare Liberalism arose following the economic collapse of 1929 when government was put to work to address the social problems that became so evident in the Great Depression. Through such measures as progressive taxation to share the wealth, regulations to improve workplace safety, and programs to protect the environment, the federal government sought to advance the common good. Welfare Liberalism held sway until the 1970s, when Neocapitalism, a reinvigorated defense of free enterprise, began its ascent. Intellectuals like Milton Friedman and politicians like Ronald Reagan argued for a reduction in federal government size and influence. The Neocapitalists convinced many that "supply-side economics" would create wealth that would "trickle down" through all ranks of society. Neocapitalism has now reigned as the dominant public philosophy for the past 30 years of American history. While it has led to considerable success in wealth creation for a small percentage of our population, its contributions to advancing the public good are less clear.

As the shortcomings of Neocapitalist ideology and the radical individualism on which it is founded have become increasingly apparent, more and more politicians and captains of industry speak in terms of seeking the public good through public/private partnerships. Whether the subject is environmental pollution, energy conservation, healthcare, or public school reform, more and more national, state, and local leaders understand the negative consequences suffered or the positive consequences missed when we fail to bring the dynamism of capitalism into productive harmony with larger societal interests. To survive and prosper today and in the future, we must find ways to balance individualism and a concern for the common good.

This pendulum between individualism and a concern for the common good swings back and forth in response to shifting political winds. Although we have a history in our country of catering to the individualistic side of ourselves, there is much room for improvement when it comes to our social side. What we need is something between individualism and communalism, between Neocapitalism and Welfare Liberalism. What we need is something akin to capitalism with a social conscience.

Meanwhile, our admiration for self-reliance clashes with the reality that not all problems lend themselves to self-reliant solutions. What to do about healthcare is but one example. The issue drives home the point that when it comes to "crunch time," most of us, just like the marshal in *High Noon,* could benefit from the assistance of others. In the words of one economist, rather than a YOYO ("you're on your own") philosophy, we need a WITT ("we're in this together") state of mind.[19]

The Ecological Perspective[20]

Ecology provides us with this much needed rationale for a "we're in this together" state of mind. It challenges us to change the way we think about ourselves in relation to one another and move from "either/or" to "both/and" ways of looking at the world. Seeing life as Herbert Spencer did—as merely survival of the fittest—denies much of what we have accomplished together in community. On the other hand, to see life as Marx and Engels saw it in *The Communist Manifesto*—"From each according to his abilities, to each according to his needs"—shortchanges our individual skills and abilities and undercuts the entrepreneurial spirit and work ethic that are keystones of a healthy economy. We are neither 300 million "billiard balls" bouncing off one another as we go about our private business, nor are we insignificant cogs in a monstrous, unfeeling governmental machine. We are—as ecology teaches us—interconnected and interdependent beings. Fulfilling lives consist of symbiotic relationships with one another that mirror this reality.

This ecological perspective is described by Daniel Yankelovich in *New Rules: Searching for Self-Fulfillment in a World Turned Upside Down.*[21] Yankelovich challenges America's prevailing "psychology of affluence," a social attitude grounded in individualism that encourages us not only to want but also to expect more of everything. This attitude is problematic, according to Yankelovich, because there are in all likelihood not enough material things to satisfy everyone, and even if there were, human fulfillment is not derived from the consumption of material goods. Fulfillment is derived from meaningful work and satisfying relationships. A psychology of affluence that creates a materialistic mind-set and an insatiable appetite is bound to be fundamentally lacking in both meaning and satisfaction over the long haul.

A healthier approach, one we might call the "ecology of service living," recognizes our interdependence and promotes human fulfillment in its sociocultural context. Obviously this is a less self-indulgent way of thinking than the psychology of affluence. A clear illustration of the ecology of service living can be found in Duane Elgin's *Voluntary Simplicity.*[22] Voluntary simplicity is "a practical expression of the compassionate understanding that our individual well-being is inseparable from the well-being of other members of the human family."[23] It means we choose to live our daily lives with some degree of conscious appreciation of the condition of the rest of the world. Elgin's perspective is appealing because it celebrates the deliberate choices of people who recognize that the psychology of affluence is self-defeating. It is neither a moral justification for acquiring more things nor is it a "me-first" philosophy. On the contrary, it calls for a much more temperate code of human conduct. The code is based on the realization that we live in a world of limits and that we are all in this world together. It is a code based on ecological insight. It warns us that if we do not replace the psychology of affluence with the ecology of service living, our long-term prospects for a fulfilling life will continue to shrink.

Service living is grounded in ecological thinking. It celebrates that part of each of us that is connected to the larger community of life. It derives its meaning from lifelong action that contributes to the health and well-being of all living things. Service living, like voluntary simplicity, means we are choosing to live our daily lives with some degree of conscious appreciation of, and responsibility for, the condition of the rest of the world. It is a way of living whose time has come.

James Madison and others instrumental in the founding of American democracy believed our form of government depended on civic virtue among its citizens. As Bellah and his co-authors wrote in the closing lines of *Habits of the Heart:*

> The tension between private interest and the public good is never completely resolved in any society. But in a free republic, it is the task of the citizen, whether ruler or ruled, to cultivate civic virtue in order to mitigate the tension and render it manageable.[24]

In the chapters that follow we introduce you to four individuals who cultivated civic virtue and exemplified service living. Each of them understood their connection to the larger community of life. Each of them contributed to the health and well-being of all living things. Each of them lived their individual lives with a conscious appreciation of the condition of the rest of the world. That they chose to live this way is testimony to the potential in each one of us to rise above our individualistic tendencies in service of the greater good.

II
Painting with Lakes and Wooded Slopes: The Democratic Artistry of Frederick Law Olmsted

...Each of you knows the name and genius of him who stands first in the heart of American artists, the creator of your own parks and many other city parks...He it is who has been our best advisor and common mentor. In the highest sense he is the planner of the Exposition—Frederick Law Olmsted...No word of his has fallen to the ground among us since first he joined us some thirty months ago. An artist, he paints with lakes and wooded slopes; with lawns and banks and forest-covered hills; with mountainsides and ocean views. He should stand where I do tonight, not for the deeds of later years alone, but for what his brain has wrought and his pen has taught for half a century.[1]

—Daniel Burnham *(lead architect of the 1893 World's Columbian Exposition in Chicago, on Frederick Law Olmsted's contributions to the success of the venture)*

In 2006, the Atlantic magazine invited ten eminent historians to develop a list of the 100 most influential figures in American history. Frederick Law Olmsted was ranked number 49.[2] Best known for his work on New York's Central Park, and revered as the father of landscape architecture in America, Olmsted contributed greatly to the quality of American life and the strength of our democracy. This chapter focuses on the ideas about American democracy and landscape design that shaped Olmsted's major work in the public sector and the life experiences that formed those ideas.

Witold Rybczynski, one of Olmsted's biographers, notes, "What laid the groundwork for his later achievements was an amalgam of sensibility and temperament, coupled with an unusual set of formative experiences."[3] We begin with these formative experiences covering the 35-year span from his birth to his engagement in planning Central Park, the work with which Olmsted is most universally associated.

The Foundation: Family, Education, and Environment

In 1822 in Hartford, Connecticut, Frederick Law Olmsted was born into the middle-class household of John and Charlotte Olmsted. Of the many fortunate events in his long life, being part of this family was chief because it set the stage for all that would follow. His father was a successful dry-goods merchant, retailing woolens, cottons, silks, carpeting, and "fancy goods" in competition with other merchants in the small but lively town. John Olmsted was a descendant of Puritans who came from England in 1632. Members of his family had worked for seven generations as farmers, traders, and merchants. They were also patriots who fought for their country in the Revolutionary War. As a successful businessman, Frederick's father was a representative of the lawyers, clergymen, and merchants who were pillars of their small communities in the early 19th century. From his father Olmsted gained a strong sense of patriotism and a commitment to advancing the common good, as well as a love of learning through reading and travel. In his father Olmsted also enjoyed the support of someone with the means to finance his numerous ventures as he struggled to figure out what he would do with his life.

When Olmsted was three, his mother died from an accidental overdose of laudanum, an opium-based pain medicine she had taken for a toothache. A little over a year later, his father remarried, and he and his wife began a new family. As the six children born to this new union began to fill the household, Frederick was sent off to school with a series of tutors. Between the ages of seven and fifteen, he moved from one school or tutor to another while spending only two extended periods at home. He was an independent thinker who rebelled against the dogmatism and rote learning dealt out by the country parsons who tutored him, and he spent much of his time reading and roaming the beautiful Connecticut countryside. He emerged from his early education with an aversion to organized religion, a conviction that slavery was wrong, and a love of self-directed learning and pastoral landscapes.

Olmsted was fortunate not only in his parentage but in his birthplace. Hartford in the early 1800s was a vital, interesting city with easy access to a beautiful countryside. When he was living at home, he got to know Hartford well. Although it had a population of only 7,000, Hartford was a vibrant manufacturing and commercial center with international trade that opened Olmsted's eyes to the world. Hartford was also intellectually alive and stimulating. It was "...no provincial backwater but a place of some intellectual consequence."[4] Young Olmsted was surrounded by people engaged in the life of the mind.

The physical environment in which Olmsted spent his youth provided him with a permanent standard of reference of a pastoral landscape. It closely resembled the English countryside he would later discover. Shortly before Mark Twain moved to Hartford in 1868, he described the town in these words: "Of all the beautiful towns it has been my fortune to see, this is the chief. Everywhere the eye turns it is blessed with visions of refreshing green. You do not know what beauty is if you have not been there."[5]

Searching for a Vocation

Olmsted struggled to figure out how he would make a living. His first effort, at age 15, was to study surveying. While he learned much about civil engineering that would later prove valuable in his landscape designs, by age 18 he was bored and ready to try something else. Following in his father's footsteps, he went to New York as an apprentice clerk for a firm that imported dry goods. He learned about bookkeeping, accounting, and office organization, and he was exposed to a city much larger than Hartford.

In 1840, New York's population was about 300,000, and the tone of the city was set by the dynamism of untrammeled capitalism. The 1811 plan for developing Manhattan Island on a grid of streets and avenues was still in the early stages of implementation. The northern part of the island remained largely rural while Lower Manhattan, where Olmsted worked, was densely built with narrow, bustling streets. The few public open spaces were poorly maintained. Across the East River in Brooklyn Heights where Olmsted lived, individual houses interspersed with open fields and woods conveyed a small town atmosphere. Residents took their leisure in the Greenwood Cemetery, an early example of a burial ground in the picturesque English style. These rural cemeteries were designed to create the illusion of a pastoral countryside and induce reflection and a sense of repose in visitors.

After working as an apprentice clerk, Olmsted decided that being a businessman was not his calling in life. He returned to his parents' home in Hartford, where he avidly pursued outdoor recreation and young women while pondering what he would make of himself. Soon he made up his mind to go to sea. This decision may have resulted from his need to do something dramatically different after months of indolence, but it was not an unreasonable choice. His family's seafaring history helped set the stage and steer Olmsted toward service as a common seaman in the China trade.

With two friends, he set sail from New York in the spring of 1843. The yearlong voyage was a valuable learning experience, primarily because it exposed him to the rough lives of ordinary working men. He suffered illness and a bad fall, endured terrible food and harsh weather, and experienced the toxic combination of a barbarous crew and an authoritarian captain. He was disgusted by the crude behavior of the crew, and he was appalled when the captain punished a young boy with 20 lashes simply for swearing. Olmsted's year before the mast shaped his thinking about civilization and barbarism and spurred his lifelong commitment to democratic principles. Writing about his experience after his return, he expressed outrage at existing seafaring conditions and proposed special schools to better prepare "greenhorn" sailors for the rigors of a life at sea. His hope was that better prepared sailors would have the capacity to serve effectively without such brutal leadership.

At 19 years of age, Olmsted had considered and rejected college, surveying, business, and seafaring. He understood his own inner strength and his great need for independence, but no clear career path had opened to him. Taking another page from his family's history, he decided to try farming. He worked for a year on farms owned by an uncle and a family friend, at the end of which he concluded that farming was indeed the answer because it entailed both healthy outdoor work and continuing education. Olmsted was experimenting with farming at a time when it was shifting from traditional practices to commercial agriculture. In this transition, business and applied science were becoming increasingly important ingredients of success. To learn science, he sat in on classes at Yale, where he joined his brother John who was studying medicine.

Bankrolled by his father, Olmsted bought a farm on Long Island. His first farm, while scenic, was marginally productive. Again with his father's help, he sold it and bought a better farm on Staten Island. Olmsted was an innovative farmer, but he never succeeded in turning a profit. After some time, he decided that the nursery business suited him better than raising crops because it was less risky. If prices dipped, he could simply leave the trees and shrubs in the ground until market prices improved. Demand for nursery stock was growing with the expanding popularity of landscape gardening. The nursery business also afforded him more leisure for reading and other intellectual pursuits. He developed his social network and got to know neighbors of wealth and influence including a son of the fabulously wealthy capitalist Cornelius Vanderbilt, poet and civic leader William Cullen Bryant, and Ralph Waldo Emerson's brother Judge William Emerson.

A Walking Tour of Europe

Travel was a lifelong source of inspiration and learning for Olmsted. In 1850, he persuaded his father to support a walking tour of Europe with his brother and one of his close friends from Yale. Instead of focusing on the usual tourist highlights, the three decided to concentrate on understanding the lives of the working class: "We all thought that it should be among those classes which form the majority of the people of a country that the truest exhibition of national character should be looked for, and that in their condition should be found the best evidence of the wisdom of national institutions."[6] Their six-month tour took them to England, France, Belgium, Holland, Germany, Ireland, and Scotland. However, it was the time in England that left the most lasting impression. England was, after all, Olmsted's ancestral home and the home of the writers he most admired. Olmsted's description of a private park in a country estate provides an early statement of the pastoral ideal that became the hallmark of his park designs:

> A gentle undulating surface of close-cropped pasture land, reaching way off illimitably; very old, but not very large trees scattered singly and in groups—so far apart as to throw long unbroken shadows across broad openings of light, and leave the view in several directions unobstructed for a long distance. Herds of fallow-deer, fawns, cattle, sheep and lambs quietly feeding near us, and moving slowly in masses at a distance; a warm atmosphere, descending sun, and sublime shadows from fleecy clouds transiently darkening in succession, sunny surface, cool woodside, flocks and herds, and foliage.[7]

As biographer Laura Wood Roper explains, Olmsted responded to the "commonplace scenery" of rural England, not to striking landscape features. The broad strokes of the theory of landscape beauty that would guide his later work were already in place. As he wrote in *Walks and Talks of an American Farmer in England* after his return to America:

> Beauty, grandeur, impressiveness in any way, from scenery, is not often to be found in a few prominent, distinguishable features, but in the manner and the unobserved materials with which these are connected and combined.[8]

England's private parks also charmed him. Yet Olmsted was chilled by the stark contrast between the lives of the landed gentry and the common farmers he encountered. As Roper recounts:

> ...Fred was not an uncritical Anglophile. His aesthetic sensi-
> bilities were charmed, his moral (sensibilities) scandalized,
> by the luxurious trappings of aristocracy. Inspecting a splen-
> didly maintained Welsh castle set in a beautiful park, he was
> enraptured by the elegance and taste of the life it typified. But
> his immediate second thought was: 'Is it right and best that
> this should be for the few, the very few of us, when for many
> of the rest of us there must be but bare walls, tile floors, and
> everything besides harshly screaming, scrabble for life?'...
> The poverty, the nearly brute circumstances, of some of the
> peasantry contrasted horribly with the ease of the well-to-do
> and shocked him deeply...Fred had no use, then or later, for
> the doctrine of laissez faire.[9]

In Liverpool, Olmsted and his companions discovered Birkenhead Park, a recently created 120-acre city park designed to create the illusion of a pastoral countryside. This discovery aroused Olmsted's interest for several reasons. First, the park was entirely man-made, an artistic creation that transformed a bland piece of property into an evocative landscape. Second, the park was explicitly designed for public use at a time when most English parklands were privately owned. The visitors he saw included people from all walks of life. He was enchanted by the park, which he saw as an engine of democracy working to relieve the misery of the poor and break down social class barriers.

The walking tour of Europe, especially the discoveries of the pastoral English landscape and the pastoral city park in Liverpool, were instrumental in shaping Olmsted's future. According to Roper:

> Although he seems hardly yet to have realized it, two absorb-
> ing interests—the one in landscape, the other in means of ele-
> vating the character and condition of the poorer
> classes—were beginning to converge to produce in him a
> compelling enthusiasm for public parks in cities.[10]

On his return to America, Olmsted was invited by the leading American landscape designer of the time, Andrew Jackson Downing, to write an article about his travels. He chose to write about his experiences in England and, in particular, Birkenhead Park. In his 1851 article he provided technical details about drainage systems and path construction, and he explained how park construction was publicly financed. He stressed that the park was created for and enjoyed by people from all walks of life, and he noted the irony that in democratic America there was nothing comparable. Downing welcomed this analysis since he had long complained about New York City's lack of public parks in comparison to London's.

In a letter written after his return to America, Olmsted reflected on what he had learned in England and its implications for government's role in seeking the common good. He did not believe that government should be limited to protecting private property and maximizing individual freedom under a laissez-faire philosophy. Instead, he thought government should encourage and support:

> ...at points so frequent and convenient that they would exert an elevating influence upon all the people, public parks and gardens, galleries of art and instruction in art, music, athletic sports and healthful recreations, and other means of cultivating taste and lessening the excessive materialism of purpose in which we are, as a people so cursedly absorbed, that even the natural capacity for domestic happiness...for the enjoyment of simple and sensible social life in our community, seems likely to be entirely destroyed. The enemies of Democracy could bring no charge more severe against it, than that such is its tendency, and that it has no means of counteracting it.[11]

Analyzing Slavery

About this time, Olmsted's friend from Yale and the European tour, Charles Brace, began to make his mark in social work. His conversations with Olmsted frequently led to high-energy debates about slavery. Between 1800 and 1850, the American slave population had tripled to a total of three million people, and new legislation allowed for the expansion of slavery in the West and required that runaway slaves be returned to their owners. Olmsted and Brace were aligned in their opposition to slavery, but Olmsted could not accept Brace's call for its immediate and wholesale abolition. Following the logic he had developed in thinking about seamen and their masters, he wanted emancipation to proceed gradually, increasing as those in bondage achieved the capacity for liberty.

As chance would have it, the editor of the newspaper that would become *The New York Times* was looking for someone who could travel through the South and inform readers about conditions there. He wanted a reporter who could be seen as an objective observer, not an abolitionist with his mind already made up. He approached Brace, and Brace recommended Olmsted.

Olmsted understood immediately that this assignment was perfect for him. He could travel, learn about new places, and by careful observation gather facts that might help to guide the country to a reasonable resolution of its great crisis.

Over the course of 14 months in 1852–1854, Olmsted made three trips to the pre-war South. He made careful observations, talked to people from all walks of life, reflected on what he learned, and filed regular dispatches under the pseud-onym of "Yeoman." His inquisitive mind and dogged attention to detail led him to thorough, if not stylish, writing. Critic Edmund Wilson found his reporting "pedestrian," but gave him high marks for digging out important information:

> He tenaciously and patiently and lucidly made his way through
> the whole South, undiscouraged by churlish natives, almost
> impassable roads or the cold inns and uncomfortable cabins in
> which he spent most of his nights…He talked to everybody,
> and he sized up everything, and he wrote it all down.[12]

Following his third and last trip to the South, Olmsted returned to his farm and began turning his collected dispatches and notes into books: *A Journey to the Seaboard Slave States* (1856), *A Journey through Texas* (1857), and *A Journey in the Back Country* (1860). Later still, he boiled down these ponderous books into *The Cotton Kingdom: A Traveler's Observations on Cotton and Slavery in the American Slave States, 1853–1861*. Published in 1861, this classic is still in print. Considered together, Olmsted's writings on the South significantly influenced the thinking of intellectuals and policy leaders in the North and Europe. Only *Uncle Tom's Cabin* had greater impact, and Harriet Beecher Stowe's famous book was a work of imagination based on one trip to Kentucky rather than months and months of careful observation and thoughtful analysis grounded in facts.

Olmsted's critique of slavery was based on its economic failures. Since slaves were in bondage, they had no incentive to work hard or efficiently. Since owners could not fire their slaves, many resorted to corporal punishment. Brutal beatings often left slaves temporarily disabled and compounded the eco-nomic failures. Fearing that training or educating their slaves would lead to discontent, owners had no incentive to upgrade their skills. Building on his analysis of seafaring, Olmsted viewed the evils of slavery as rooted in deep systemic causes. In Olmsted's analysis, the fundamental flaws in slavery tended to corrupt all of Southern society. Slave labor was coerced and slaves resisted by working slowly and carelessly, and this approach permeated all social classes: "You notice in all classes, vagueness in ideas of cost and value, and injudicious and unnecessary expenditure of labor by thoughtless manner of setting about work."[13]

In luring his friend Frederick into reporting on the South, Brace was hop-ing the experience would move Olmsted's stance on abolition closer to his own. He succeeded. What Olmsted learned from firsthand encounters with individual slaves changed his thinking about their "capacity for liberty" for the better. By the end of the newspaper series, his views about abolition had hardened considerably, and he called unequivocally for giving the slaves the opportunity to show they could "make a good use of the blessing of freedom."[14]

Following his fact-finding travels in the South, Olmsted returned to his Staten Island farm in 1854 and began work on the books. Increasingly writing, not farming, commanded his interest and energy. After seven years, his farm was still not self-supporting—his father was contributing the equivalent in today's currency of over $30,000 per year—and his writing was beginning to pay. With his father's blessing, Frederick turned the farm over to his brother John and moved to New York.

Through friends, Olmsted met the young publisher who had purchased *Putnam's Monthly Magazine* with the idea of featuring American authors rather than the British authors favored by rival *Harper's*. They struck up a partnership that had Olmsted serving as managing editor. In this role, Olmsted worked directly with many of the leading American writers of the day including Melville, Thoreau, Emerson, Stowe, and Irving. Although *Putnam's* met with critical acclaim, it was chronically short of money. Compounding his financial difficulties, Olmsted had to borrow from his father to publish his first book on his travels in the slave states. His increasingly pro-abolition position also led to his involvement in the struggle over whether Kansas would be a free-soil or slave state. He even got into arms dealing, buying "a mountain howitzer together with fifty rounds of canister and shell…five hand grenades, fifty rockets, and six swords" to help Kansas free-soilers defend themselves against pro-slavery raiders from Missouri.[15]

Central Park

Now in his mid-thirties, Olmsted was living in New York, trying to make a success of his magazine and books, while continuing to wrestle with the question of what he would do with his life. His most pressing concern was how he would begin to make a livelihood so he would not have to continue to rely on his father for financial help. Through a chance meeting with a friend who was serving on the recently created Board of Commissioners for Central Park, Olmsted was invited to apply for the superintendent's position in August of 1857. The superintendent would organize laborers and park police for this 800-acre park that had been authorized for some years but did not yet have a master plan.

Olmsted saw a chance to do something that would utilize his varied skills and address his major interests. He also saw a way of solving his persistent financial problems. In his application letter, he called attention to his knowledge of European parks and park operations and the practical knowledge of

soils and vegetation management he had gained during ten years of farming.
He sought and received support for his application from almost 200 leading
citizens including the influential editor, William Cullen Bryant, whose 1844
editorial had been instrumental in the park's creation. Olmsted won the job, but
after infighting among the commissioners he was offered an annual salary of
only $1,500, not the $3,000 he was expecting. He considered his options—
none good—and took the job.

Olmsted walked into a tough situation as superintendent of the Central
Park project. The push for a major park in New York City had begun with
elites interested in protecting their property values, providing themselves with
a place for carriage rides, and enhancing the city's standing relative to London,
Paris, and the other European centers of commerce and culture. Working people protested and called for small parks close to where they lived and worked
that were suited to the pastimes they enjoyed.[16] The New York legislature had
authorized the city to acquire the land in 1853. Although five years had passed
and $5 million in taxpayer money had been spent, all they had was a rough
piece of land and a preliminary plan. Progress on park development had been
tied up in political maneuvering, and pressure to move forward was intense.
The workforce Olmsted was to manage consisted of 500 to 600 men. Many
owed their jobs to political patronage and their loyalty to the Chief Engineer,
Colonel Egbert Ludovicus Viele. Viele's credentials were questionable; he was
not trained as an engineer, and his military service was not in the Corps of
Engineers but fighting Mexicans and Indians in the Southwest. He sized up
Olmsted and concluded this "literary gent" posed no threat to his power base.

Viele made a big mistake in underestimating Olmsted. The breakthrough
came when the park commissioners assigned Olmsted, not Viele, the task of
planning how to handle drainage on the property. With his study of engineering, his farming experience, and the knowledge from his educational travels to
Europe, Olmsted produced a viable drainage plan. His performance on this and
other jobs earned Olmsted the trust of the commissioners. They soon raised his
salary to $2,000. They also gave him the authority to remove unproductive
workers and hire new ones to expand the workforce to 1,000. Four months into
his new job, he was showing the chief engineer just how smart and tough he was.

To appreciate the challenges Olmsted faced at Central Park, it is important
to know something of the social conditions in New York City at that time.
Roper notes that Olmsted took charge of the largest public works project in the
city at a time when the social order was in "dark eclipse."

> (The social order) had been declining through the 1840s,
> when a million and a half European immigrants had poured
> into the city, many of them to crowd and stagnate in its sordid
> and degrading slums. There gangs, native and foreign born,

fought and slaughtered each other; in better neighborhoods footpads, pickpockets, prostitutes, and beggars operated busily; at fires, companies of volunteer firemen brawled with rival companies and other rowdies. Gang members, firemen, criminals, each with his vote to sell, had palpable influence in the political organization of the city, especially Tammany Hall, and were little disturbed by the police.[17]

The physical site of Central Park was as challenging as the city's social and political order. When Olmsted was first hired as superintendent, Viele arranged for a tour of the land that would become the park, assuming the "literary gent" would be defeated by what he found there. The park site was a rough piece of land with rock outcrops, thin topsoil, wetlands, and traces of the 1600 families that had been evicted: small houses, pigpens, slaughterhouses, and bone-boiling works.

Viele had prepared a plan for Central Park, but it had not been adopted. Political wrangling was the chief reason for the delay, but another reason was the lobbying against it carried out by architect Calvert Vaux. Vaux had been raised and educated in London. He came to America at the behest of the prominent landscape gardener Andrew Jackson Downing, who wanted an architect to work with him designing country estates. Following Downing's untimely death in a steamboat accident, Vaux moved to New York City. He considered himself Downing's heir, and he proclaimed that Viele's plan lacked grace and style and would violate Downing's vision.

Through Downing, Vaux and Olmsted had met some years earlier. When the Central Park commissioners decided to open a design competition, Vaux persuaded Olmsted to work with him. For Olmsted, the partnership offered access to the design expertise he lacked and the chance to pay off his debts and perhaps garner another raise. For Vaux, it offered first-hand knowledge of the site and a connection with someone currently favored by the commission. Working evenings and weekends for months, the partners and several assistants prepared their plan, which they called Greensward. It was the last of 33 entries submitted. The fact that it was a day late was overlooked.

Greensward was a revolutionary design for an American city park. In one of his periodic reports to the commission, Olmsted spelled out the vital importance of Central Park to a future New York City built out on the 1811 grid plan. The park would offer citizens from all walks of life—and in particular workers boxed in by their jobs as well as buildings—a place of striking contrast for respite and restoration. In his words:

> The time will come when New York will be built up, when all the grading and filling will be done, and when the picturesquely-varied, rocky formations of the Island will have been converted

into foundations for rows of monotonous straight streets, and
piles of erect, angular buildings. There will be no suggestion
left of its present varied surface, with the single exception of
the Park. Then the priceless value of the present picturesque
outlines of the ground will be more distinctly perceived, and
its adaptability for its purpose more fully recognized. It therefore seems desirable to interfere with its easy, undulating outlines, and picturesque, rocky scenery as little as possible, and,
on the other hand, to endeavor rapidly and by every legiti-
mate means, to increase and judiciously develop these particularly individual characteristic sources of landscape
effects.[18]

The site of the park that would fulfill Olmsted's vision was challenging to
say the least. Although 800 acres in size, it was only a half-mile wide. Creating
the illusion of the country in the city required great foresight and care. In addition, like all competitors, Olmsted and Vaux had to address the design require-
ments, which included "...three large playing fields, a parade ground, a flower
garden, a lookout tower, and a music hall or exhibition building" among other
features.[19] In the absence of a clear organizing principle, their design would be
a jumble, as indeed many of their competitors' designs were. Olmsted and
Vaux found their essential design principle in Downing's vision that the park
would provide varied opportunities for visitor experiences: "Pedestrians would
find quiet and secluded walks when they wished to be solitary, and broad alleys
filled with thousands of happy faces when they would be gay."[20]

Olmsted and Vaux began with the required promenade later called the
Mall. Instead of making it a primary feature as most others in the competition
did, they made it relatively small and set it at a slight angle to the surrounding
grid to de-emphasize its importance. Similarly, their plan for the tower was to
keep it small and not detract from the natural scene they were striving to create. The most innovative part of their plan was how they handled the require-
ment of accommodating four or more transverse roads. Preventing cross-park
traffic from destroying the pastoral atmosphere was the key to the personal
restoration they sought. They planned to blast out eight-foot deep trenches and
build the roads in them to remove them from the sight of park visitors. Throughout the Greensward plan, they designed views that were diagonal to the grid,
which drew visitors' attention to the green landscape within the park rather
than to the nearby buildings Olmsted predicted would someday border the narrow park on all sides.

Greensward won the contest. Although Downing had strongly influenced
the city's initiative as well as the views of Olmsted and Vaux, Greensward did
little more than pay homage to his vision for the park. Breaking from Down-

ing's vision of a park with exciting structures like London's Crystal Palace, Olmsted and Vaux took their cue from the rural cemeteries and Birkenhead Park and created the illusion of a pastoral countryside that would provide maximum contrast to the surrounding city.

With the prize in hand, Olmsted realized staying with the project through construction and beyond was essential. He understood the commissioners' propensity for meddling with the Greensward design and for cutting costs at the expense of quality. He knew it would be years before victory could be declared, and he wanted Vaux's help in this long but necessary struggle. Vaux bowed to Olmsted's persuasive powers and their partnership continued. Though enduring and highly successful, the partnership required work and sacrifice on both sides. For example, soon after the competition was completed, the commissioners added "Architect in Chief" to Olmsted's title of Superintendent. Vaux was the certified architect, and Olmsted's new title irritated him. However, he chose not to make it an issue because he recognized that Olmsted was far better suited for the managerial and organizational issues the person in charge would have to handle.

Issues started cropping up almost immediately. Two politicians on the commission proposed major changes. Like Viele, they underestimated Olmsted and thought they could roll over the Greensward plan through political machinations. Olmsted responded by enlisting the help of his literary friends who attacked the proposed amendments in the press and knocked down ideas that would have compromised the plan. Interestingly, Olmsted and Vaux did adopt one of the proposals—using bridges at the crossings of different kinds of paths—to reduce conflict between pedestrian and carriage traffic.

Although the Greensward vision was for a natural park in the heart of a growing metropolis, Olmsted and Vaux freely modified the existing landscape. The largest rock-crusher in the world operated at the site and the transverse roads were blasted out. In the middle of the 19th century, however, humans and animals, not machines, did most heavy work. At its height, the labor force at Central Park numbered 3,500. To manage this huge crew, Olmsted recruited highly qualified engineers, gardeners, and other experts. Chosen on the basis of their expertise rather than their political loyalties, and given freedom to do their jobs, these men did great work and were highly loyal to the boss. Olmsted hired people more skilled than he was in specific areas, and he learned from them, but he was unchallenged in his mastery of the big picture.

In 1859, after two years on the job as Superintendent, Olmsted collapsed. The long intense days, evenings, and weekends caught up with him, and were compounded by personal matters. During his work on Central Park, his beloved brother John had succumbed to tuberculosis and died suddenly while in Europe. Olmsted could not be with him at the end. Two years after John's death, Olmsted married John's widow, Mary, thereby keeping his promise that he would take care of John's family. The marriage was good, but it also added to his responsibilities. His energy flagging, he sought and gained permission for a six-week vacation. He sailed to Europe where he continued his education in park design and management. He traveled not to relax but to learn, and by learning he recharged his batteries.

He revisited Birkenhead Park, which had played such a pivotal role in leading him toward his life's work. He went on to study English country estates and parks in France and Belgium. Everywhere he went, he talked with experts, built his understanding of park design and operations, and made contacts he could draw on later. One of his major discoveries was the work of the 18th century architect and landscape gardener Lancelot "Capability" Brown. The romantic landscape theorists Olmsted had read in his youth disparaged Brown's voluminous work—over 170 private parks and gardens in England—as old-fashioned. Olmsted, however, found Brown's designs in perfect harmony with his own sense of appropriate public park design. Brown worked on a large scale, and he kept it simple. His parks were works of art. To achieve the effects he sought he dug out lakes, rounded off land, and composed clusters of trees. Even though he was not reluctant to modify the original landscape, he always began his design work by attending to what nature was capable of—hence his nickname, "Capability." He was also practical and realized that fancy designs involved high maintenance costs and that maintenance failures in the future would undercut a park's value. In the work of Capability Brown, Olmsted found precedent and vindication for the landscape design approach he had come to on his own.

Olmsted returned from Europe revitalized and full of new information. However, he found himself constrained by the Central Park commission due to mounting concerns about cost overruns, many of which resulted from the commission's own decisions. As the commission concentrated on containing costs, they chose Andrew Haswell Green—a man of substance who had a highly successful career and had backed Olmsted in the early days at Central Park—to manage the budget. This decision placed Olmsted on a collision course with someone as smart and determined as he was. Olmsted found his authority challenged, his judgment called into question, and his time and energy depleted responding to Green's demand that all expenditures, no matter how small, be justified.

As his working relationships at Central Park deteriorated, additional problems befell Olmsted. Driving a carriage pulled by a new horse he was thinking of buying, he fell asleep and dropped the reins, and the horse ran out of control. The carriage hit a lamppost and Olmsted was thrown onto a boulder. His leg was broken in three places. Doctors recommended amputation to prevent gangrene, but Olmsted was so weak he might not have lived through the amputation, so all they could do was wait and hope for the best. Against long odds, Olmsted survived this trauma. He emerged with a pronounced limp but refused to allow it to slow him down. Compounding his misfortunes, eight days after his accident his youngest son died of infant cholera. Throughout it all, he struggled to manage his debts.

The U.S. Sanitary Commission

As Olmsted soldiered on at Central Park, he continued developing his literary career. *The Cotton Kingdom* was published in 1861. Olmsted had a strategic reason for pushing to complete the book. He understood that the South's economy and the institution of slavery depended on cotton, and the primary market for cotton was England. He wanted to influence British public opinion and provoke policy actions that would undercut slavery.

His book was well-received and may have influenced British policymakers, but the currents of history overwhelmed everything. Abraham Lincoln was elected president, Jefferson Davis was elected president of the "Provisional Government of the Confederate States of America," Fort Sumter was attacked, and soon the Civil War was fully engaged.

A patriot from a patriot's lineage, Olmsted wanted to volunteer for service, but his health would not permit it. Through an acquaintance he was asked to become the chief executive officer of the United States Sanitary Commission, an organization formed to monitor the Union army's health and sanitary conditions and advise the Medical Bureau. He secured a leave of absence at half pay from the Central Park commissioners and plunged into his new job. At age 39, he was hoping this service would help him find his mission in life. Like many Northerners, Olmsted expected a short war of a month or two at most. His work would be a refreshing break from the grind at Central Park.

Olmsted's optimism was soon crushed. Visiting troop encampments around Washington, he was appalled by the army's disorganization. He found the Medical Bureau unprepared and unresponsive to the recommendations of a civilian. He had no time to nurse the alarm he felt, however, as the First Battle of Bull Run (First Manassas) erupted. Despite their numerical advantage, the Union troops were routed. Olmsted recruited a talented staff to conduct a study of the sanitary conditions of the Union army before, during, and after the battle. He prepared a report showing that poor leadership and lack of advanced preparation caused "demoralization" and failure. The army leadership refused to release the report, but the president of the Sanitary Commission was sufficiently impressed to order major changes that strengthened Olmsted's hand.

Building on his study of the First Battle of Bull Run, Olmsted launched a thorough investigation of the sanitary conditions throughout the Union Army. His hand picked staff visited regimental camps and hospitals and observed the conditions of troops being transported by rail. Using a 180-item checklist Olmsted prepared, they focused on disease prevention. As his staff collected essential data, Olmsted battled with the recalcitrant Medical Bureau and produced a report that solidified the Sanitary Commission's legitimacy and role.

One of Olmsted's major accomplishments during the Civil War was the creation of the Hospital Transport Service. Collecting his own small fleet of ships, he developed a system for transporting wounded soldiers to hospital ships. His description of the scene following the battle of Fair Oaks station provides a sense of the dire conditions he faced:

> At the time of which I am now writing, Monday afternoon [two days after the battle], wounded were arriving by every train, entirely unattended or at most a detail of two soldiers to a train of two or three hundred of them. They were packed as closely as they could be stowed in the common freight cars, without beds, without straw, at most with a wisp of hay under their heads. They arrived, dead and alive together, in the same close box, many with awful wounds festering and alive with maggots. The stench was such as to produce vomiting with some of our strong men, habituated to the duty of attending the sick & wounded of the army.[21]

During the year Olmsted's *ad hoc* transport service was in operation, his ships carried 8,000-10,000 casualties with a death rate of 165 per 1,000, half the rate experienced by the British in the Crimean War. Development of the army's ambulance service reduced the need for the Hospital Transport Service, and Olmsted moved on to other things.

As at Central Park, Olmsted's tour of duty in the Civil War demonstrated his leadership qualities. He set a standard for hard work, as recorded by one of his staff:

> He works like a dog all day and sits up nearly all night... doesn't go home to his family (now established in Washington) for five days and nights together, works with steady, feverish intensity till four in the morning, sleeps on a sofa in his clothes, and breakfasts on strong coffee and pickles![22]

He assembled an outstanding professional and volunteer staff and won their loyalty. Katherine Wormeley, one of his team, expressed her feelings in these words:

> Did I say somewhere that Mr. Olmsted was severe, or some- thing of that kind? Well, I am glad I said it, that I may now unsay it. Nothing could be more untrue; every day I have

understood and valued and trusted him more and more. This expedition, if it has done no other good, has made a body of lifelong friends. We have a period to look back upon when we worked together under the deepest feelings, and to the extent of our powers, shoulder to shoulder, helping each other to the best of our ability, no one failing or hindering another. From first to last there has been perfect accord among us; and I can never look back to these months without feeling that God has been very good to let me share in them and see human nature under such aspects. It is sad to feel that it is all over.[23]

California and Yosemite

With his role in the Civil War winding down and Olmsted casting about for something more inviting than returning to the struggle at Central Park, fate led him to California. In 1863, a group of New York businessmen purchased the huge Mariposa Estate in California—the site of the fabulous "Mother Lode" gold vein—and offered Olmsted the job of manager. For a salary of $10,000 and 100 shares of company stock per year, he would be in charge of an operation covering 70 square miles in the Sierras that included six mines, two towns, a railroad, and 7,000 people. The businessmen wanted Olmsted's answer quickly.

Olmsted found this opportunity attractive. He would make enough money to pay off his debts, assure the welfare of his family, and perhaps become sufficiently wealthy that he would be taken more seriously in public affairs. On the other hand, he struggled with his conscience. The man who had hired and supported him at the Sanitary Commission exhorted him to continue public service instead of working for businessmen interested only in profits. In the end, his sense of responsibility to his family won out and he accepted the offer. He had no social safety net, and if accident or illness prevented him from making a living, his wife and children would become charity cases.

Olmsted sailed for California in the fall of 1863, and his family followed six months later. Upon arriving at the Mariposa Estate, he examined the company's finances. What he found shocked him. In anticipation of putting the estate up for sale, previous managers had deferred maintenance to pump up profits, and they had held back mining some of the most promising veins until just before the sale. Instead of the $60,000 to $100,000 per month advertised, profits were $25,000 per month. Olmsted moved quickly to cut costs. He cut workers' wages from $3.50 to $3.15 per day, which led to a strike. He hired substitute workers and stared down the strikers. The balance line began to improve, and Olmsted was optimistic.

Once again, however, he experienced health problems. Olmsted felt fatigued and learned he had an enlarged heart and needed to take life easier. He accepted the doctor's advice, slowed down, and for the first time he enjoyed leisure with his family. Although his friends back East thought of him as being in exile, Olmsted described himself as "never happier." Among his recreational excursions, he was introduced to Yosemite Valley and the Mariposa Grove of Giant Sequoias. The valley—about ten miles long and one mile wide—had been discovered by white men 13 years earlier and had become well-known through the photographs, paintings, and travelers' accounts. Camping in the valley near the 2,425 foot Yosemite Falls, Olmsted recorded his impressions:

> We are camped near the middle of the chasm on the bank of
> the Merced, which is here a stream meandering through a
> meadow…like the Avon at Stratford—a trout stream with
> rushes & ferns, willows & poplars. The walls of the chasm
> are a quarter of a mile distant, each side—nearly a mile in
> height—half a mile of perpendicular or overhanging rock in
> some places. Of course it is awfully grand, but it is not fright-
> ful or fearful. It is sublimely beautiful, much more beautiful
> than I had supposed. The valley is as sweet & peaceful as the
> Avon, and the sides are in many parts lovely with foliage and
> color. There is little water in the cascades at this season, but
> that is but a trifling circumstance. We have what is infinitely
> more valuable—a full moon & a soft hazy smoky atmosphere
> with rolling towering & white fleecy clouds.[24]

Rybczynski analyzes Olmsted's impressions and relates them to Central Park:

> The unique and affecting charm of Yosemite, as Olmsted per-
> ceptively noted, is that it is both wilderness and landscape.
> The craggy vastness of the chasm is older than any human
> presence, yet the valley floor appears comfortably domesti-
> cated. Olmsted appreciated this curious contrast; he and Vaux
> had created precisely this effect in Central Park, where the
> wilderness of the Ramble was side by side with pastoral
> meadows.[25]

Earlier that year, the federal government had granted 20 square miles of Yosemite Valley and 4 square miles of the Mariposa Grove of giant sequoias to California for "public use, resort and recreation."[26] A key ingredient in the groundbreaking 1864 grant was the prospect of tourism development. The natural features were wonders of nature. What could be more American than finding a way to make a profit from them? Olmsted was appointed to a commission charged by the governor with developing a plan for Yosemite. Not surprisingly, he assumed leadership of the commission in fact if not in title.

Forces beyond Olmsted's control led to the demise of the Mariposa Company at this time. Whether planned by Olmsted's employers or the inevitable result of previous mismanagement, the company rapidly moved toward bankruptcy. Olmsted struggled as things fell apart. Personally, however, he came out ahead. His time at the Mariposa Company enabled him to clear his debts and build some financial security. It also led to design commissions in San Francisco that burnished his reputation as a landscape architect and helped settle his long search for his calling in life.

Although no longer the manager of the company, Olmsted remained on-site for six months hoping that somehow he would receive full payment of his second year's wages. He began writing and gathering material for a planned book on civilization in America. He believed the frontier barbarism he had seen in the South and at Mariposa was an inevitable result of the process of pioneering:

> Pioneering required self-reliance, yet self-reliance often degenerated into self-indulgence and greed. Self-reliance was also accompanied by an exaggerated sense of personal honor, lawlessness, and profligacy.[27]

For Olmsted and others in the 19th century, civilization "described an enlightened state of virtuous and intellectual development… (and was)…the best condition of mankind." Civilization's polar opposite, barbarism, was the plight of immigrants who in moving had lost "all the old roots of local lore and historic feeling, the joints and bonds that minister nourishment."[28] For Olmsted, a strong social contract was the key to the good life. The term he chose to express this ideal social contract was "communicativeness," which he defined as a "…combination of qualities which fit (a person) to serve others and to be served by others in the most intimate, complete and extended degree imaginable."[29] As Roper further explains:

> He called it 'communicativeness,' and by it he distinguished the civilized man from the barbarian. Communicativeness involved recognizing, and acting consistently on the recognition, that one had an essential community of interest with other human beings, regardless of regional, class, economic, color, religious, or whatever differences. Barbarism, conversely, assumed that those not distinctly allied to one's self by some clearly identifiable bond were alien, contemptible, and fair game. Communicativeness had no room for narrowly

selfish interests, whether of individuals or groups or classes....
Translated into political terms, communicativeness was the
essence of democracy, and Olmsted was democratic to the
marrow.[30]

While closing out his stay at Mariposa, Olmsted completed the plan for
Yosemite. Having conceived Central Park as a place where ordinary citizens
could experience temporary relief from the pressures and limitations of a capitalist economy, and having struggled for years against proposals for man-made
intrusions that would detract from that experience, Olmsted's organizing principle at Yosemite was clear—to preserve the natural scenery and the visitor
experiences it could engender.

Simply preserving Yosemite's spectacular features—its "freaks of nature"—
was not what Olmsted had in mind. The area's cliffs, waterfalls and giant trees
were wonderful, but what was special about Yosemite was the overall compo-
sition and character of the valley:

> There are falls of water elsewhere finer, there are more stu-
> pendous cliffs, there are deeper and more awful chasms, there
> may be as beautiful streams, as lovely meadows, there are
> larger trees. It is in no scene or scenes the charm consists, but
> in the miles of scenery where cliffs of awful height and rocks
> of vast magnitude and of varied and exquisite coloring are
> banked and fringed and draped and shadowed by the tender
> foliage of noble and lovely trees and bushes, reflected from
> the most placid pools, and associated with the most tranquil
> meadows, the most playful streams, and every variety of soft
> and peaceful pastoral beauty. The union of deepest sublimity
> with the deepest beauty of nature, not in one feature or
> another, not in one part or one scene or another, not in any
> landscape that can be framed by itself, but all around and
> wherever the visitor goes, constitutes the Yosemite the great-
> est glory of nature.[31]

In his plan for Yosemite, Olmsted identified two factors that had led to the
ground breaking federal action. The first and less important was the "pecuniary
advantage" that might arise from tourism. The success of the Swiss tourism
industry and a public garden in Bavaria designed to attract tourists had amply
demonstrated the revenue-generating potential of nature tourism. When
Yosemite became readily accessible, it might draw tourists from around the
world and become an important part of California's economy.

A more important reason was the enhancement of the public good that would derive from citizens from all walks of life enjoying Yosemite's splendors:

> It is the main duty of government, if it is not the sole duty of government, to provide means of protection for all citizens in the pursuit of happiness against the obstacles, otherwise insurmountable, which the selfishness of individuals or combinations of individuals is liable to interpose to that pursuit.[32]

What benefits might citizens—especially those with little power or wealth—derive from spending time in a place like Yosemite? Olmsted drew on science to make his case:

> It is a scientific fact that the occasional contemplation of natural scenes of an impressive character, particularly if this contemplation occurs in connection with relief from ordinary cares, change of air and change of habits, is favorable to the health and vigor of men and especially to the health and vigor of their intellect beyond any other conditions which can be offered them, that it not only gives pleasure for the time being but increases the subsequent capacity for happiness and the means of insuring happiness. The want of such occasional recreation where men and women are habitually pressed by their business or household cares often results in a class of disorders the characteristic quality of which is mental disability, sometimes taking the severe forms of softening of the brain, paralysis, palsy, monomania, or insanity, but more frequently of mental and nervous excitability, moroseness, melancholy, or irascibility, incapacitating the subject for the proper exercise of the intellectual and moral forces.[33]

In Europe, the rich and powerful had long ago seized the choicest natural sites for their private recreation. In America, still in the first century of its experiment in democracy, Olmsted believed ordinary citizens should have access to natural places conducive to what he called the "contemplative faculty." In *Mountains Without Handrails,* Joseph Sax explains Olmsted's "distinctive hypothesis...the basis of his prescription for the national parks":

> In most of our activities we are busy accomplishing things to satisfy the demands and expectations of other people, and dealing with petty details that are uninteresting in themselves

and only engage our attention because they are a means to
some other goal we are trying to reach. Olmsted does not suggest that gainful activity is a bad thing, by any means; only
that it offers no opportunity for the mind to disengage from
getting tasks done, and to engage instead on thoughts removed
from the confinement of duty and achievement. He calls this
the invocation of the contemplative faculty.... For Olmsted
the preservation of scenery is justified precisely because it
provides a stimulus to engage the contemplative faculty.[34]

Olmsted believed nature had the power to engage the contemplative faculty,
where "...the attention is aroused and the mind occupied without purpose, without
a continuation of the common process of relating the present action, thought or
perception to some future end... [thereby]...engaging the moral perceptions and
intuitions."[35] He acknowledged that not everyone is ready to experience nature's
benefits, but he believed that, properly prepared, all citizens are capable of it. The
duty of government in a democracy is to help them achieve it. As Sax explains:

It is unquestionably true, but it is not inevitable, he said, '...that
excessive devotion to sordid interests,' to the constant and
degrading work upon which most people are engaged, dulls
the aesthetic and contemplative faculties. It is precisely to
give the ordinary citizen an opportunity to exercise and educate the contemplative faculty that establishment of nature
parks as public places is 'justified and enforced as a political
duty.' ...Behind his rather archaic vocabulary, and his pseu-
doscientific proofs, lies a prescription for parks as an important institution in a society unwilling to write off the ordinary
citizen as an automaton.[36]

Olmsted's argument about the value of parks in American democracy led
him to his primary managerial principle for Yosemite, a special place Congress
had treated differently from the rest of the public domain:

The first point to be kept in mind then is the preservation and
maintenance as exactly as is possible of the natural scenery;
the restriction, that is to say, within the narrowest limits con-
sistent with the necessary accommodation of visitors, of all
artificial constructions and the prevention of all constructions
markedly inharmonious with the scenery or which would
unnecessarily obscure, distort or distract from the dignity of
the scenery.[37]

Lured back to New York City by Calvert Vaux to work on Prospect Park in Brooklyn, Olmsted left California without presenting his report to the legislature. Other members of the commission scuttled it, and it was lost to history until discovered in 1952 by biographer Laura Wood Roper, who published the report and described its importance in these terms:

> In this document Olmsted elaborated, for the first time in America, the policy underlying the reservation by government to the public of a particular, and fine, scenic area; and he gave it a general application. In short, he formulated the philosophic base for the establishment of state and national parks.[38]

The robust philosophical principles Olmsted set out in his Yosemite plan continued to guide his landscape design and urban planning work throughout his career. As Sax concludes in his analysis of Olmsted's plan for public recreation management at Niagra Falls, Olmsted had a bedrock commitment to democracy:

> To understand Olmsted's views it is essential to keep in mind that he was a republican idealist. He held, that is to say, to what we generally call democratic values. He believed in the possibility of a nation where every individual counted for something and could explore and act upon his own potential capacities. He feared, and he condemned, the nation of unquestioning, mute, and passive followers. The destruction of Niagara's scenery appalled him, not simply because the place was ugly, but because old Niagara was a symbol and a means for the visitor freely to respond to his experience. The trouble with the new Niagara was that it had returned, with its leading and hurrying of visitors and with its commercial entertainments, in the guise of free enterprise, to the same contemptuous disregard of the individuality of the visitor that had characterized the aristocratic, condescending spirit of Europe.
>
> …The commercialized Niagara was enjoyable, it provided a service for the leisure time that citizens had to spend. Olmsted's Niagara plan called for some sacrifice of that service in order to provide a place designed to engage the contemplative faculty and to encourage the visitor to set his own agenda. He believed these were opportunities that citizens of a democratic society ought to want to provide themselves.[39]

A Life Well-Lived

His work in California completed, Olmsted returned to New York to establish an enormously successful landscape architecture firm. Vaux, his nephew John Quarles Olmsted, his son Frederick Law Olmsted, Jr., and others joined him in this venture. Between 1857 and 1950, Olmsted's firm completed over a thousand landscape designs for clients and communities across the United States. They designed the grounds of 355 school and college campuses including Yale, Johns Hopkins, Michigan State, Notre Dame, and Stanford.[40] They designed the landscaping for the Biltmore Estate in Asheville, North Carolina, and Olmsted hired Gifford Pinchot as its forester, thereby helping launch scientific forestry in the United States. Carrying on Olmsted's legacy, his son Frederick Law Olmsted, Jr. helped write the 1916 law that established the National Park Service.

Toward the end of his career, Olmsted served as senior mastermind in the creation of the 1893 World's Columbian Exposition in Chicago. The exposition was a monumental undertaking that involved many of the most admired architects in the country and employed a labor force of as many as 20,000 workers. When fully operational, the fair alone consumed three times the electricity used by the entire city of Chicago.[41] The fair was a huge success. At a time when the entire population of the United States was 63 million, the exposition drew 27 million visitors over the course of six months.[42]

Biographer Roper deserves considerable credit for Olmsted's current high standing in American history. Writing in 1973, before Olmsted's work gained renewed appreciation, she puzzled over why he was not considered an American hero. She concluded:

> He fits no generally accepted heroic mold. He was not a courageous soldier, a towering statesman, an intrepid explorer; he was not even an underdog triumphant over odds. He was, instead, something not at all glamorous: a well-bred intellectual, a determined patriot, a practical and foresighted artist, a brilliant executive, and a man of multifarious interests and enormous industry. Nor was he self-aggrandizing: he believed that the function of the fine arts, especially the one he practiced, was to uplift and refresh the spirit of others, not to express the personality of the artist.[43]

Frederick Law Olmsted died in 1903 at the age of 81, having made profound and enduring contributions to the quality of American life. The circumstances of his formative years were favorable to a life of accomplishment, but many people have enjoyed equally or more favorable circumstances and made much less of them. Persisting in his search for his calling through a series of ventures that ended in failure, and enduring physical and psychological disabilities (depression) that would have defeated lesser individuals, Olmsted continued throughout his life to develop big ideas and work toward putting them into action. He built those big ideas through wide-ranging and persistent reading and discussion, and he continually tested his thinking in exchanges with other thinkers. He took risks and learned from his failures. Throughout his life, he focused his attention on advancing the common good and securing the promise of democracy. He embodied service living.

III
Employing Sympathetic Knowledge: Jane Addams of Chicago's Hull House

If "ignorance is bliss" then what is an education? Jane Addams would have given us an answer to that question. She would have said that education is having sympathetic knowledge. Sympathetic knowledge is the idea that humans can learn about one another in terms that move beyond propositional or theoretical knowledge.[1] Rather than learning facts, knowledge is gained through openness to social change and "disruptive action." Sympathetic knowledge provides the rationale behind social action and Jane Addams was the epitome of social action and service living.

Addams is acknowledged by many modern disciplines as a central contributor to the way people thought about the world at the beginning of the 20th century. She was one of the most famous women in the United States and certainly one of the most beloved Americans in the world.[2] Her work has been associated with fields such as sociology, social work, juvenile justice, philosophy, and recreation. In the last 20 years of her life, she was an outspoken pacifist and closely associated with the peace movement. Although the founding of Hull House in Chicago in 1890 was not the first settlement house in the United States, it was the most famous due to the public charisma and notoriety of Jane Addams.[3]

In this chapter we describe Addams' life and her passion for public service. Terms that describe her include community organizer, reformer, pragmatist, social theorist, author, urban planner, recreation worker, feminist, and pacifist. While these descriptions provide a framework for examining Jane's life, she did not want to be labeled since she believed getting the work done was more important than labeling the people who did it.

Despite her numerous accomplishments and prestigious awards including the Nobel Peace Prize, Jane did not know in her young adulthood what she wanted to do with her life. She felt "absolutely at sea" for many years because of severe depression and terrible back problems.[4] Reconciling the expectations of "ideal womanhood"[5] and her calling to public service was necessary. She also realized that nothing could be accomplished without engaging others in the vision of a just world and having the sympathetic knowledge that "the good we secure for ourselves is precarious and uncertain until it is secured for all of us and incorporated into our common life."[6]

Biography as Amalgamated Experiences

Understanding how an individual's life is shaped requires an examination of formative experiences. Although this chapter is arranged around the images associated with Ms. Addams' life, a brief biographical sketch provides a context for understanding the life of one of the most dedicated social reformers in American history.[7]

Jane Addams was born in 1860 in Cedarville, Illinois. She was the youngest of eight children and at the age of two, her mother died. Her sister died when she was six and her father remarried when she was eight. He brought a stepmother and her two sons into the family, which clearly changed the family dynamic.

Jane's father was the center of her early universe. She always gave her father credit for molding her life. He was a successful businessman, won election to the Illinois State Senate on a Republican ticket focused on anti-slavery, and was a friend of Abraham Lincoln who called him "My Dear Double D'ed Addams." Jane's father was the richest man in the county and had built the largest house. This story provides great insight into Jane's later life:

> One day when she was seven years old, Jane asked her father
> why some of the children in town lived in dirty little houses
> crowded close together. He explained that many people were

poor and uneducated, with few opportunities in life. According to her autobiography, Jane decided at that spot that "When I grow up I should of course have a large house, but it would not be built among the other large houses, but right in the midst of horrid little houses like these."[8]

Jane's father had an extensive library collection and paid Jane a nickel for each book she read.[9] She was fascinated with heroes, although most of whom she knew as heroes were men. One book that captured her heart was Louisa May Alcott's *Little Women*. The book offered two kinds of heroes: the devoted mother and the independent girl. She identified with Jo, the independent girl, as the hero most like herself who had heroic ambitions.[10]

Jane's father tutored her in politics and history and emphasized individual rights as well as community stewardship by the virtuous elite. She held this philosophy about stewardship throughout her life. She believed in cooperative democracy and her father taught her the importance of hard work and ethical conduct. Religion, however, was not the basis for these efforts. Jane's stepmother also taught her about social graces, the arts, and how wealth could buy culture.[11]

Jane had an infection as a child that left her with a slightly curved spine. This defect led to Jane's sense that she was an ugly girl, an "ugly duckling" as she described herself.[12] Despite the poor health that she experienced throughout much of her life, Jane persevered as a child and into her adulthood and tried never to let her back troubles prevent her from participating in any type of activity. Thus, while she had wealth and status from her family background, she also was confronted with personal and family doubts and complexities.

Jane entered the Rockford Female Seminary (now called Rockford College) near her home when she was 17. She wanted to go east to Smith College but her father thought going there was too far away. She was encouraged to become a missionary at Rockford but a religious life did not appeal to her. She resisted the school's Christian evangelism and avoided its feminizing and domesticating influences. She knew she wanted to help people but she was not sure how. She excelled in the classroom and served as president of her class all four years.[13] Although revered by her classmates, Jane was a private and somewhat emotionally distant individual, similar to her father. She was, however, a superb student and named valedictorian of her class. In her valedictory speech she talked about the potential to do great things. "We stand united today in a belief in beauty, genius, and courage, and that these can transform the world!"[14]

Soon after graduating from college, Jane's doting and supportive father died and her stepmother expected her youngest unmarried daughter to be her companion. Along with her stepmother, Jane moved to Philadelphia and enrolled in the Women's Medical School. She left after a semester, however, realizing that dull medical texts were not for her and that the family situation and her personal health were not conducive to study. She had an operation on her back, which relieved some of her problems, but as an unexpected result of the surgery she was told she would never have children.[15]

Over the next two years, Jane grew depressed not knowing what to do with her life. She had inherited from her father what in today's currency would be equal to one million dollars,[16] but she knew the "privileges of culture and wealth"[17] would not make her happy unless she could share with others. She struggled with her expected family roles and with the social issues she encountered. She did not want to accept the typical female role of domesticity expected of women in that period of history. She always had been intellectual and active, but she did not know where to place that energy. Her doctor finally prescribed a two-year trip to Europe with her stepmother to restore her happiness.

In Europe, Jane explored galleries, palaces, and cathedrals. She also saw the poverty and desperate condition of many urban areas. She began to question the inequities between rich and poor as well as the role of women in society. On a second trip to Europe, she was accompanied by her good friend from the Rockford Seminary, Ellen Gates Starr. They toured Toynbee Hall, which was an experimental project in an impoverished area of London. Founded in 1884, it was the world's first "settlement house." Educated young men actually lived (i.e., "settled") in the area and offered classes in literacy, art, and other activities to community members. When she returned to Illinois, Jane decided to establish her own settlement house in the slums of Chicago.

During the summer of 1889, eight years after graduating from college, Jane and Ellen elicited support for a settlement project from churches, civic organizations, and wealthy citizens in Chicago. Chicago had one million residents and was the second largest city in the United States after New York City.[18] Chicago had many arts and entertainment opportunities, but Chicago also had some of the worst slums in the nation. Jane and Ellen searched for a large house in the "midst of horrid little houses."[19] She found her mansion on Halsted Street in industrial Chicago. The original owner was Charles Hull so the mansion became known as Hull House.

Jane initially rented the second floor and a large reception area on the main floor. The owner eventually donated the entire building to the cause. Other friends warned Jane and Ellen that they would be robbed and forced to give up their dreams, but Jane and Ellen were undeterred. With Starr's contacts and Addams' public charisma and status as the educated daughter of a former state senator, Hull House soon was up and running. Jane's own family, however, saw her work as "abandonment of filial duty."[20]

Jane and Ellen had no real idea how to proceed but Jane believed that they must be good neighbors. Jane also believed that their work should be nonsectarian and focus on social cooperation. Good neighbors would celebrate each other's joys as well as help each other endure hardships. She believed Hull House could serve the community and teach people about joyful living. She also knew she wanted to address the inequality among people and educate them about things they had in common as well as about the qualities that made them unique.[21] Most of the people initially served were from southern and eastern Europe who had fled poverty and political oppression. Little did these refugees know that they would face the same kind of prejudice and discrimination in America.

✱As the neighbors got used to the women at Hull House, they began to stop by. Jane and Ellen ran a nursery for workers' children in the day time and then began inviting their neighbors for activities like parties, dancing, and Shakespeare readings in the evening. Jane was often shocked by the isolation of these immigrant neighbors. Few had ever been to a museum or a city park.

Privileged and idealistic young women and men also came to Hull House.[22] Jane was particularly interested in getting a community of activist women together. Mary Rozet Smith, for example, was a rich Chicagoan and devoted supporter of Hull House who became Jane's lifelong partner. Julia Lathrop worked to improve the conditions of children and established Chicago's first juvenile court. Dr. Alice Hamilton endeavored to reduce threats to public health and Florence Kelley fought for safety standards and humane working hours for immigrants. These people were all part of the progressive reform movement and were committed to social change in whatever ways were possible.

Over the years Hull House expanded to include an art gallery, coffee house, and gymnasium, serving thousands of people. Eventually it consisted of 13 buildings that encompassed an entire city block. Children came to play, parents studied English, immigrants taught dancing and folk songs from their native countries, and Jane and her companions offered friendship, relaxation, and hope for their neighbors.

Kindness, however, was not enough as it became clear to Jane that political action was needed to change the industrial and health problems of Chicago and the nation. Some neighborhoods in Chicago were filthy and garbage collection was atrocious in the area around Hull House. Half the children born in the city did not live to their fifth birthday because of unsanitary conditions. When all else failed, Jane got herself appointed garbage inspector to ensure that the problem was addressed. In time, other individuals oversaw this collection and the death rate dropped in Hull House's ward.[23]

The first ten years at Hull House were exhausting with many projects demanding Jane's attention.[24] From being depressed and somewhat disabled, Jane became an energetic young woman with a purpose and goals. Jane's life then changed from a given life to her chosen life.[25] In addition to the daily work at Hull House, letters had to be written and funds had to be raised. Jane's inheritance helped to get Hull House off the ground, but it did not allow her to expand the settlement. Her supporters contributed in many ways through their influential contacts (mostly women) in Chicago. However, when the "hard" issues of child labor and shorter work days (i.e., 8 hour days) were raised, some of Jane's supporters began to view her efforts with suspicion. They feared that the Hull House residents were troublemakers who wanted to keep honest business people from making a profit.

As time went on, Jane found herself involved in numerous important causes. One was her opposition to war. She believed that war was never the answer and advocated for founding an international court that would resolve all disputes between nations. She also opposed the United States entering into World War I. Despite vicious criticism, she stood her ground. When the war was over, she visited the battlefields and offered aid to both the American allies and to the defeated Germans.

Although Jane did a great deal of traveling in her later years, and although her peace efforts consumed her, the work of Hull House continued. The neighborhood changed to Mexican and African American citizens who had needs similar to the earlier European residents. Jane never retired from this work, but she spent more time in her later years in her summer home in Maine or with friends in Arizona. Members of Franklin D. Roosevelt's New Deal administration also frequently contacted her for advice.

Despite all the accomplishments of Hull House, Jane became unpopular with many people during the 1920s because of her peace efforts, and she was vilified for a time as "the most dangerous woman in America." Through it all, most of her friends remained faithful to her. As the bitterness of the war years faded, some people even admitted that perhaps she had been right. Her dedication to peace year after year won many people's respect.[26]

In 1931, Jane Addams was awarded the Nobel Peace Prize, which was one of the greatest honors ever bestowed on an American woman. The Prize was given for both her efforts at Hull House and her work for peace. She donated all the prize money to the Women's International League for Peace and Freedom, which she had helped found. The Peace Prize committee cited her for her "expression of an essentially American democracy of spirit"[27] as well as her work at Hull House "…where anyone desiring it may obtain aid…here is a mother for everyone. She is not one who talks much, but her quiet personality creates an atmosphere of good will."[28] The Nobel citation read further:

> Carrying on this social work amongst people of widely different nationalities, it was natural that she should take up the cause of peace, and for nearly twenty-five years she has been its faithful spokesman….She founded a big organization of women [to work for peace]. At times she had public opinion

against her, but she did not give up and she won at last the place of honor she now holds.[29]

At the age of 70, Jane was still juggling many responsibilities. She claimed that as long as she could hold a pen, she could do meaningful work.[30] Many people considered the Nobel Peace Prize to be her crowning achievement, but Jane was not ready to retire. Her health, however, had never been great and continued to decline until she died of incurable cancer in Chicago in 1935 at the age of 74. Thousands of friends filed by the coffin that stood in the Hull House reception room.[31] Impassioned eulogies were given, and strong women and men with children stood weeping for the friend they had lost.[32] Jane Addams was buried in Cedarville, Illinois, where she had spent her childhood. An editorial in a Los Angeles, California newspaper noted:

> Only with time can the stature of Jane Addams be measured...
> she was honored by eminent societies in many countries....
> When Abraham Lincoln died, her father told her, "the greatest
> man in the world has passed away." Little did the 5-year-old
> dream that 70 years later men and women in every land
> would say, when the news of her death was flashed along the
> cables, 'the greatest woman in the world has passed away.'[33]

This short biography touches on the numerous contributions Jane Addams made to the progressive era through her service living. Her efforts can be understood further by describing the significant nonmutually exclusive roles she played throughout her life.

Community Organizer

When it came to Hull House and the myriad activities surrounding it, Jane Addams was the epitome of a community organizer. She surrounded herself with committed people (mainly elite women) who were willing to be teachers and activists. One of Jane's strengths was her ability to guide others to be creative, socially conscious, and hardworking. She was adamant about sympathetic knowledge. Jane feared that education sometimes resulted in people losing a sense of empathy. This fear was based on Jane's own postbaccalaureate experience.

Because of Jane's early exposure to different classes of people, she argued for a spirit of mutual respect in all endeavors. Although she wanted to help others, she also wanted them to help one another. Jane believed that work across classes was necessary if social problems were to be solved. She believed that equality and education were anything but mutually exclusive. The melting pot was not her idea of how American society should progress, but rather that people should respect one another and their cultures. Jane also believed in the fundamental goodness and interdependence of people. The experience of others was as important as her own. She summarized her views about community organizing this way: "Social advance depends as much upon the process through which it is secured as upon the result itself."[34] Thus, for both the residents of Hull House and their neighbors, Jane wanted to help people make contributions to their ventures by enabling them to act on their own ideas. She believed that if the best results were to be achieved, people had to be afforded the liberty of action.

The community organizing that Jane undertook was a means of demonstrating her beliefs about democracy. She understood democracy as both a form of socially engaged (i.e., service) living and a framework for social morality. The upshot of this community organization was reflected in how action led to reform.

Reformer and Pragmatist

The latter part of the 19th century was an important period for the reform movement in the United States. Although the list of Jane's accomplishments was long and she had a wide range of concerns, she fortunately lived in a time when many Americans were concerned about bringing equity and dignity to individuals, especially in urban areas. Jane Addams' life coupled progressive thought with pragmatism and activism. She gave the progressive movement ideological coherence and was a humane but challenging voice. "Action indeed," she said, "is the sole medium of expression for ethics."[35]

Although both theory and experience were important, Jane put experience before theory. She did what needed to be done to address people's needs. For example, as noted previously, she became the garbage inspector for the 19th Ward of Chicago when it was needed. She was the Vice President of the National Women's Trade Union League (1903), helped found the National Association for the Advancement of Colored People (1909), was elected first woman President of the National Conference of Charities and Corrections (later known as the National Conference of Social Work, 1909), served as the Mediator in the Chicago Garment Worker's Strike (1910), was elected First Vice President of National American Woman Suffrage Association (1911-1914), became the first head of the National Federation of Settlement and Neighborhood Centers (1911-1914), seconded Theodore Roosevelt's nomination at the Progressive Party convention (1912), and helped found the American Civil Liberties Union (1920), to mention only a few of her major leadership roles.[36]

In serving these many causes, Jane was known for trying to avoid organizational squabbles. She felt her contributions to Hull House and her philosophical writings were her most important pragmatic contributions. Her recoil from contentious issues was both a virtue and a bane. Some people applauded her insistence on mediation in all matters of conflict. Others resented her cool distancing. Getting the work done organizationally, however, was shared with many others. She empowered the residents of Hull House to take on their own social advocacy roles. Each was encouraged to identify a community need and then address it through their work. These residents were, in turn, encouraged to involve other community members in self-advocacy and action.

Jane Addams often said that she hoped a day would come when Hull House or other settlement houses like it would no longer be needed. She believed the government should take over this charitable work.[37] Had she lived through the Great Depression, she would have seen how the government did become involved in helping people through programs like the Social Security Act, U.S. Housing Authority, Food Stamp Program, and Job Corps, which were similar to the services Hull House provided.

Although Jane Addams supported many causes, she advocated most for one: democracy won through peaceful means. She strove throughout her life to change industrial urban America to a peaceful democratic social ideal. Jane was a social critic who offered alternative plans of action through her service living to lead to better outcomes.

Social Theorist

Jane Addams could have been a brilliant scholar, but she chose to live in the "real" world. "Social progress, education, democracy, ethics, art, religion, peace, and indeed, happiness, must be found in day-to-day experiences,"[38] she said. Nevertheless, her writing reflected obvious scholarly threads through observations, analyses, perspectives, and calling her audiences' attention to bigger pictures. As a social theorist, Jane believed that only the democratic process could create a stable, healthy society, and only a peaceful process can produce democracy's goals. She often theorized that only peace and democracy can bring peace and democracy. Jane also believed that the threat to democracy was caused by the extremes of classes.[39]

Jane Addams was also one of the early philosophers and theorists about play. She was familiar with G. Stanley Hall's theory of recapitulation and argued that more parks and playgrounds were needed so children could have an outlet for their energies.[40] She did not believe, however, that theories were necessary to aid people in the self-expression and self-assertion promises of play.

Education is associated with Jane Addams since formal education and schools were something she addressed directly, although not necessarily successfully. Because of her progressive views, Jane was asked to serve on the Chicago Board of Education from 1905 to 1908. Her attempts at educational reform were not met positively, mainly because of her support of teachers' unions.

Jane was more successful in sharing her views about adult education and lifelong learning. She believed education should be connected to everything in life. Some of these ideas may have originated from her frustration with having a college degree and no apparent way to use it in her young adulthood.

Jane's ideas about education and life were similar to John Dewey's.[41] Dewey and Addams both disseminated their thinking through writing. Both published books at the same time, and who influenced who is difficult to say. The two were intellectual soul mates who associated frequently, and Dewey dedicated one of his books to Jane after her death. He was fascinated with Hull House and Addams' ideas.[42] In some ways, Dewey was more often associated with thinking and theory while Addams was more often associated with doing and activism. The philosophy of progressive education as a place where culture was democratized so everyone could share in the sciences and arts was central to both Addams' and Dewey's thinking. In her speeches, Jane delivered the message "that cultured people had a responsibility as citizens to help immigrants and other working people seek a fuller social and intellectual life."[43]

Another element of Addams' social theory related to how education was necessary for the middle classes to understand the plight of the poor.[44] Observation and analysis were a part of what her settlement colleagues did, and this information was used for reports and speeches to help the middle class understand the working poor and to be able to better help them. Jane did not believe in either the melting pot theory or Social Darwinism. She felt the mixture of cultures made everyone's lives better and that becoming one homogeneous American culture was not a particularly good idea. She also opposed Social Darwinism and did not believe the fittest should survive and the rest go under. Jane was opposed to elitism in any way. A unique aspect of her public service was that she recognized how theory and practice had to go together. Her writing reflected this union.

Author

For those of us who were born many years after Jane's death, one of her gifts to us was her prolific writing. Much of the writing came from the numerous speeches she gave all over the world beginning in the early 1900s. The timeless and compelling nature of her writing lives on as she was the author of 11 books and countless papers. In 1910, she wrote her first book and then published on a variety of topics thereafter. In the first decade of the 20th century alone, almost 150 articles appeared under Jane's by-line[45] and it is estimated that she published between 500 and 2000 articles in her lifetime.[46, 47]

Many aspects of Hull House led to its national prominence, but Jane's writings and leadership style were also highly significant. Her literary contributions, in particular, made Hull House stand out from numerous other settlement houses in the United States at the beginning of the 20th century. Her writings also helped create a constituency to support legislative reform across the country.

Jane Addams gave the progressive movement a voice and provided ideological as well as pragmatic coherence to it.[48] Her use of language enabled her to become the conscience of the nation. Jane was, unarguably, the most effective and prolific writer of her generation of reformers. Her examination of social democracy and the issues facing urban America are relevant to this day.

Urban Planner and Recreation Worker

Jane Addams is claimed by a number of turn-of-the-century social movements as a significant contributor to the health of urban areas. Social workers see her as their pioneer as do juvenile justice workers. Recreation professionals also claim her for her involvement in the early Playground Movement. Although the notion of a recreation worker or professional did not exist in Jane's day, she is associated with many of the ideals relative to urban recreation.[49]

One of her major contributions concerned youth and recreation services. Addams believed that the instincts of youth for enjoyment expressed through play were a vital social force.[50] She believed play contained the seeds of culture and democracy. Furthermore, Jane advocated that cities should take over the function of providing pleasure for people.[51] With industrialization, reduced work hours, and increased prosperity, Jane described how people would have more leisure than they had ever had before. In her book about youth and the city, Jane stated:

> Only in the modern city have men concluded that it is no longer necessary for the municipality to provide for the insatiable desire for play. In so far as they have acted upon this conclusion, they have entered upon a most difficult and dangerous experiment.[52]

Jane considered public recreation to be a means for bringing people together. Recreation programs could be used to organize and structure social life. Play could be an antidote for the loneliness and solitude that urbanization brought.[53] Although the amusement and socializing that occurred in saloons and dance halls was not horrible, Jane believed neighborhoods ought to offer more social opportunities as an alternative to commercial establishments, especially for young people. She was always looking for ways to channel youth's energy in positive ways. Jane felt that "to fail to provide for the recreation of youth, is not only to deprive all of them of their natural form of expression but is certain to subject some of them to the overwhelming temptation of illicit and soul destroying pleasures."[54]

Although Hull House was for everyone, Jane was particularly concerned about the plight of children in cities. She was involved in the formation of the Juvenile Protective Association, which met at Hull House. This association pressed for social centers, recreation rooms, public gardens, and bathing beaches that could be pleasurable and amusing within a supervised environment. Her analysis of juvenile court records showed that young people broke laws because they were in search of adventure and self-expression. She organized children into groups that were a combination of classes and clubs. She wanted to arouse their imaginations and give them opportunities to develop independent social relationships:

> '...the value of social clubs,' she stated, 'broadens out in
> one's mind to an instrument of companionship through which
> many may be led from a sense of isolation to one of civic
> responsibility, even as another type of club provides recre-
> ational facilities for those who have had only meaningless
> excitements, or, as a third type, opens new and interesting
> vistas of life to those who are ambitious.'[55]

Jane was involved with the first public playground in Chicago established in 1893. For the first 15 years, Hull House administered this playground until it was given to the city playground commission. She helped found the Playground Association of America in 1906 and was elected Vice President of that early national organization. Hull House also provided inspiration for the early development of the Chicago Park District.[56] These efforts underscored Jane's belief that the purpose of the Play and Recreation Movement was to unite city dwellers and help them express their individuality. She clearly saw recreation as a means for re-creation.[57] She believed that through play and recreation children and adults could overcome differences in language, religion, dress, and manners. A full play life for children could evolve into greater satisfaction in adult life. In essence, she saw the possibilities of transforming the power of people through recreation.[58]

Addams also saw the arts as part of the wholeness of human life and believed the arts released imagination that leads to understanding and appreciation.[59] Furthermore, culture was not only about learning but also about enjoyment.

> '...to feel the mind of the worker,' she said, 'to lift it above
> the monotony of his task, and to connect it with the larger
> world, outside of his immediate surroundings, has always
> been the object of art.'[60]

People themselves, however, had to be responsible self-advocates for those changes, not settlement or recreation workers.

Hull House used recreation to accomplish many goals. Although those of us interested in the public service aspects of parks and recreation know the influence that Jane Addams had on the profession, she is not often associated with these contributions in most biographical analyses. Her contributions to the Playground as well as the Parks and Recreation Movement are only mentioned tangentially. Nevertheless, Jane's plans for democratic urban areas were clearly tied to issues of equity and dignity through recreation and cultural opportunities for youth and adults. In addition to her work with the Playground Association of America, she was also Vice President of Campfire Girls. This association further demonstrated her commitment to education and recreation opportunities for all, with a special emphasis on girls and women.

Feminist

During the late 1800s, few careers were open to women. For the most part, ideal womanhood meant that holding a job was not proper for a woman.[61] A woman's place was in the home raising children. Girls would often excel in college but then come home to find that they could not put their education to practical use. Like many girls of her time, Jane found herself wondering how to resist this ideal and make an important contribution to society. She wanted a career more than a husband, but she struggled with these feelings given the social mores of the time and the socialization she had received that her first duty as a woman was to her family.[62] These types of concerns typically mark the initial resistance to social norms associated with feminism, although Jane never considered herself a feminist.

In retrospect, however, Jane Addams was clearly an ardent feminist. Her feminism was evident not only in how she made decisions in her life but also in her support and promotion of women throughout her life.[63] She emphasized women's strengths and not men's prejudices, which is a form of feminism often referred to as cultural feminism. She wanted to awaken women to their own power and obligations for humanity. She wanted women to see the importance of their traditional values in changing the masculine world. Jane acknowledged gender differences and believed that the virtues of women were necessary to inform, complement, and enlarge the ideas of men. She also felt that Hull House provided an opportunity for young women (like herself at one time) to have an opportunity for creative service. Hull House was a co-educational settlement house because Jane believed that males in the neighborhood needed to be able to relate to other men. However, Hull House was mostly a woman's space.

Jane was not a leader of the women's movement but an exemplar:

I am not one of those who believe—broadly speaking—that women are better than men. We have not wrecked railroads, not corrupted legislatures, not done many unholy things that men have done; but then we must remember that we have not had the chance.[64]

Pacifist

In the early years of the 20th century, Jane became active in the peace movement and was an important advocate of internationalism. She was involved with the International Congress of Women at The Hague in 1915 and maintained her pacifist stance even after the United States entered World War I in 1917. She worked untiringly with the Women's Peace Party, which became the Women's International League for Peace and Freedom (WILPF) in 1919. She was the first president of WILPF. This group continues to exist today and remains active in promoting peaceful solutions to international conflicts. A unique position of this organization is that peace alone is not the goal, but peace and freedom. Both are necessary and Addams always advocated for peace and democracy in the same sentence.

The imbalance of power in political relations, class relations, gender relations, and race relations was always on Jane's mind. She did not believe that the power of one group over another could possibly lead to peace. Social progress must be built on generous spirits and peaceful conduct. Whether internationally or in urban areas, Addams believed that citizens could engage in peaceful processes of change and achieve democratic ends once they recognized the fundamental human similarity in all people's hopes, desires, and fears.[65]

Jane was unwavering in her advocacy for peace. She was adamant about the need for mediation to avoid war and grounded her social activism in pacifist principles.[66] This view, especially during World War I, transformed her public image. She sacrificed her status as a beloved female figure to stand up for her pacifist beliefs. Her critics saw her as both a dangerous traitor as well as a silly, sentimental woman who had no business interfering with the international affairs of men. In fact, she was expelled from the Daughters of the American Revolution.[67] She lost some friends during the war but continued to be actively involved in peace issues and made many new friends.

Although Jane generally did not believe in separate organizations for women, she felt women needed to unite in the peace movement to counter men's thinking related to matters of war. She believed that most women really cared more about life than most men. Her views, however, were often unpopular. For example, one man stated in an editorial in response to her stance on peace:

In the true sense of the word, she is apparently without education. She knows no more of the discipline and methods of
modern warfare than she does of its meaning. If the woman
conceded by her sisters to be the ablest of her sex, is so readily duped, so little informed, men wonder what degree of
intelligence is to be secured by adding the female vote to the
electorate.[68]

Although Jane remained active in Hull House throughout her life, the
years after World War I were focused primarily on issues of international peace
and freedom. As Elizabeth Dilling wrote:

Jane Addams has been able to do more probably than any
other living woman to popularize pacifism and to introduce
radicalism into colleges, settlements, and respectable circles.
The influence of her radical protégés, who consider Hull
House their home center, reaches out around the world.[69]

Integrating Sympathetic Knowledge

These images of Jane Addams supplement an understanding of her life's work.
The roles she played address the sympathetic knowledge that she possessed
and the service living she encouraged in others. Jane Addams is best known for
her combination of writing, settlement work, and international efforts for world
peace. In many ways, she was a small town girl who reformed city life. Spe-
cifically, Jane was a woman of both words and action. She was a social theorist
as well as a social reformer. The goal of her life's work was to bring equity,
dignity, and peace to urban life and she was successful through what might be
described as "public charisma."

Addams integrated sympathetic knowledge as the rationale behind social
settlements.[70] This knowledge was of importance to the neighbors of Hull
House as well as to the residents that lived there. This idea also related to "lateral progress" or the belief that for authentic progress to take place, it must be
experienced in a widespread manner rather than by a privileged few. This idea
was not structured by authority but derived from participatory processes and
service living.

If being radical means challenging existing structures of power, then Jane
Addams was one of the most radical thinkers and doers of her era. She consis-
tently sought to make society better. She saw social progress as important for
all, not just for the richest, brightest, and most capable. Her radical pragmatism
also had a strong feminist tone since she gave voice to women's experiences,

addressed women's issues, and thought democracy was only possible if both men and women participated.

Jane Addams epitomized lifelong learning. She was not afraid to learn from others (e.g., Toynbee House in London), and she was always ready to share with others through her day-to-day contact, writing, or public speaking. She believed lifelong learning was a critical component of an engaged citizenry. Furthermore, Jane was not afraid to admit her mistakes. She saw mistakes as opportunities for growth.

Jane Addams personified social action. She was a public leader because she acted on her vision of the world with lifelong consistency. She believed that to be educated meant that one must lead a life of service. Jane knew that social environments could limit or liberate people and she chose to find ways that were liberating. By placing her reputation on the line when expressing her unpopular pacifist beliefs, she paved the way for world peace advocacy that many people continue to follow to this day.

If Jane Addams reappeared in the United States right now, what would she think of our progress as a nation? While urban blight and international conflict continue to exist, one wonders how much worse it might be if more than 100 years ago Jane Addams had not devoted her life to service living and effecting social change. Her leadership would certainly be helpful today. If we take her lessons to heart, we will recognize that each one of us has the ability to contribute to the lateral progress to which she aspired. Each one of us can develop the sympathetic knowledge necessary to enable us to move forward in promoting peace and democracy through service living at home and abroad.

IV
A Wilderness Pathfinder: Benton MacKaye and the Appalachian Trail

Benton MacKaye was born in 1879, just seven years after Yellowstone was designated our country's first National Park and three years before the first land was set aside for what eventually would become our National Forest system. MacKaye lived through two world wars, the Great Depression, 20 U.S. presidencies, and the first Earth Day. His 96 years spanned the most pivotal events in American conservation history—the setting aside of vast tracts of public land, the creation of federal land management agencies to oversee the steward-ship of those lands, the establishment of policies and procedures for managing those lands for the benefit and enjoyment of all Americans, and the rise of watchdog environmental organizations to keep tabs on those same land man-agement agencies. Benton MacKaye had a hand in many of these events. More importantly, his forward-looking vision of how the American landscape should be cared for continues to offer direction and inspiration to planners, policymak-ers, and natural resource advocates alike in creating a just society and a more livable world.

MacKaye conceived of the Appalachian Trail and helped inspire the legions of volunteers who built and continue to maintain and manage it. He was co-founder and president of the Wilderness Society, and he was arguably the world's first regional planner. At various times he was a progressive, social-ist, conservationist, environmentalist, and proponent of world government. Although he defies simple categorization, there is no doubt that MacKaye helped shape the public estate in the United States, the wilderness movement, and the planning profession. He was both literally and figuratively a trailblazer in the fields of conservation and regional planning. His circle of friends and colleagues read like a "who's who" of conservation heavyweights including Gifford Pinchot, Aldo Leopold, Bob Marshall, Howard Zahniser, Harvey Broome, and Harold Anderson. Although not as well-known as many of his contemporaries, MacKaye's influence was nonetheless far-reaching. He pro-moted environmental justice decades before the term was coined, and he wrote about suburban sprawl before most of the world realized it existed. More importantly, MacKaye proposed effective solutions that remain applicable today.

In this chapter, we describe Benton MacKaye's life, ideas, and impacts. We begin with a brief biography and then explore his work as a progressive activist, the conceiver of the Appalachian Trail, a father of the wilderness movement, and his influence on regional planning including his self-titled field of "geotechnics." We conclude by examining his unusual "career" as an inde-pendent scholar and mentor, his unconventional life, the major influences that led to living that life, and his lasting legacy.

Biographical Sketch[1]

Benton MacKaye (rhymes with "eye") was born in Stamford, Connecticut. He was one of six children in an educated and ambitious family of reformers who valued big ideas. His paternal grandfather was a Civil War colonel and self-made man who amassed considerable wealth as a prominent well-connected attorney. At one point he was a partner of Millard Fillmore, who would become President of the U.S. MacKaye's grandfather was also an abolitionist and social reformer who had been a leader of the Underground Railroad in New York. MacKaye's maternal grandparents were devout Baptists; he a minister and she a principal of a women's seminary and an author of biographies of missionaries. His father, Steele MacKaye, was a noted playwright and organizer of stage and other theatri-cal productions, although he was rarely at home and was never a financial success.

When Benton's grandfather died in 1888, the MacKaye wealth passed on to other relatives leaving Benton's side of the family nearly penniless. They moved to their remaining property, a modest home they called "The Cottage" in the small idyllic New England town of Shirley Center, Massachusetts. Ben-ton lived and worked there intermittently for the rest of his life. A friend called MacKaye's early family influences the "MacKaye Inheritance." "The best argument I ever saw for an aristocracy of birth is a family which preaches democracy....Theirs is a conspiracy to further the happiness of nations...That is the MacKaye inheritance—plays, novels, acting, scientific research, 'fun, fishing, and philosophy' for all the world...It is in their blood."[2]

Young Benton did not do well in school. In many ways he educated himself, preferring his personal "expeditions" in the hills around Shirley Center and learning on his own terms. While wintering in Washington, DC at the age of 12, he spent nearly every day in the Smithsonian Institution where he eagerly took notes, sketched, and was befriended by museum staff. Most importantly, he attended lectures by the great explorers of his day, whose stories and exploits captivated his attention and inspired him tremendously. Things got more difficult, however, when Benton's father died in 1894. The family's tenuous financial situation and other circumstances led the MacKayes to live a nomadic existence for a period of time. The family moved from Washington, DC (where two of his brothers had modest federal positions that helped support the family), to New York City (which Benton described as "that horrible place"), and back to Massachusetts.

In hopes of following in the footsteps of his brothers who were students at Harvard, Benton began to get serious about his education. He dropped out of traditional school and crammed for the Harvard entrance exams, which he just barely passed when he was 17. He lived a Spartan existence at Harvard, but he had two pivotal experiences during his undergraduate years that significantly affected his future. First, two of his professors changed the way he viewed the world. Geologist William Morris Davis professed "the earth as a habitable globe" for all living things. (Decades later MacKaye referred to that perspective as his "guidepost No. 1" and continued to use Davis's *Physical Geography* text as a key reference throughout his career). Davis also gave MacKaye the perspective that landforms like rivers and mountains had a "life history" measured in a geologic time frame, which greatly influenced how he viewed landscapes thereafter. The second professor was geologist Nathaniel Southgate Shaler, a friend of Gifford Pinchot and John Wesley Powell, and a proponent of George Perkins Marsh who was arguably America's first environmentalist. Shaler instilled a concern about the social implications of progress in MacKaye as well as the important role of leisure and solitude, which would also become key elements in MacKaye's worldview. Davis and Shaler were among the first of many mentors, committed colleagues, and patrons who helped shape this young idealist's thoughts and career path.

The second pivotal experience during MacKaye's Harvard years was a wilderness trek in New Hampshire with two classmates. This trek, which he later called his "journey of Ulysses," was his first true wilderness experience. The ten days they spent bicycling to the mountains and hiking the high peaks fueled his growing passion for rural landscapes, wilderness, and trails. The most memorable part of the trip was their climb up Mount Tremont amidst huge thunderstorms, an experience which biographer Larry Anderson says, "forever changed the way he responded to the world around him."[3] They spent all day traversing large "blow down" areas in driving rain with lightning striking close enough to shock them, then spent a cold, wet night near the summit. MacKaye rose before dawn and was awestruck by spectacular views of the highest peaks in New England, the valleys full of clouds, and the sun rising beyond. This day of revelation sent cold chills up his back. The experience was heightened further when a black bear surprised them and they saw soaring eagles later in the morning. This trek, and other backcountry experiences in the years to follow including two summers working as a camp counselor, began to forge in Benton a conviction about the importance of wild country and the experiences people could have there.

Benton graduated from Harvard in 1900. After an unsatisfying stint as a tutor in New York City, he returned to Harvard in 1903 to become the first graduate of the Harvard School of Forestry. In 1905, he was hired as a forest assistant for the newly created U.S. Forest Service, where he worked on and off in various positions for more than a decade. Those early years in the Forest Service were exciting and inspiring, with charismatic Chief Forester Gifford Pinchot creating a first-of-its-kind organization and advocating a conservation philosophy of natural resource use "for the greatest good for the greatest number for the greatest time." MacKaye also briefly taught forestry at Harvard where he became involved in the Harvard Socialist Club. This time was heady at Harvard, called by some the "Harvard Renaissance," and MacKaye was one of the young faculty members in the thick of it. His contract at Harvard was not renewed, possibly because of his left-wing politics and his increasingly activist role in national conservation issues.

MacKaye returned to the Forest Service and carried out a variety of responsibilities over time. His first assignment involved assisting private forest owners in adopting modern and sustainable forestry practices. Due in part to his unpublished book, *A Theory of Forest Management,* he became a U.S. Forest Service "forest examiner" and moved to Washington, DC where he undertook a series of special assignments that helped further refine his perspective on resource management and the role of natural resources in shaping communities. His Forest Service travels took him to Kentucky where he saw the southern mountains for the first time, and to Wisconsin, Michigan, and Minnesota where he witnessed firsthand the devastation of the "cutover" districts that private timber companies had clear cut and left as a landscape of stumps and slash. While conducting timber surveys in the Pacific Northwest, MacKaye was also profoundly affected by seeing the immediate and deadly aftermath of the "Everett Massacre," a labor dispute between timber company owners and workers in Washington State.

MacKaye's work gradually evolved from technical forestry to forest policy initiatives designed to refocus forest management to more directly benefit local communities. This shift led him to an assignment with the U.S. Bureau of Labor Statistics where he published his utopian *Employment and Natural Resources,*[4] which advocated federally planned communities on public lands where residents would draw their livelihood from sustainable management of nearby public natural resources such as forests.

MacKaye and his activist associates in Washington, DC became involved in many progressive campaigns and soon referred to themselves as the "Hell Raisers." Through these activities he met women's suffrage activist Jessie "Betty" Hardy Stubbs. They married in 1915. Along with their efforts on behalf of women's suffrage, the "Hell Raisers" actively campaigned against the United States' involvement in World War I, and some of them, including Benton and Betty, even volunteered their services to the Bolshevik government in Russia and offered to move there.

In 1920, MacKaye became an editorial writer for the socialist *Milwaukee Leader,* where he honed his writing skills and joined the Socialist Party. But he and his wife soon relocated to New York City. Betty's health had deteriorated dramatically from overwork and stress. After an acute "attack of nervous depression" she committed suicide in 1921 by jumping into the East River. MacKaye never fully recovered from the loss, rarely spoke of it again, and remained a bachelor the rest of his life.

At the urging of his older brother and through the generous support of close friends, MacKaye was propelled by the tragedy of his wife's suicide into a period of focus and productivity. In 1921, he wrote his now famous article in the *Journal of the American Institute of Architects*[5] proposing the Appalachian Trail and a bold system of associated communities and programs. He and his closest associates embarked on a carefully planned strategy of publicizing his ideas and mobilizing local efforts. These efforts resulted in the formation of the Appalachian Trail Conference (ATC) in 1925 with MacKaye serving as its first official "Field Organizer." Through the coordination of the ATC and the efforts of a growing number of affiliated organizations, the Appalachian Trail was completed from Maine to Georgia in 1937.

In 1923, MacKaye helped form the Regional Planning Association of America (RPAA), a small but influential group that was active for about a decade. The RPAA challenged the prevailing practices of the planning profession, promoted concepts related to the "garden city" tradition, and worked to expand planners' perspectives. He completed his most substantial published work, *The New Exploration: A Philosophy of Regional Planning,*[6] in 1928, which articulated some of the most important concepts of the RPAA.

During the 1920s and 1930s, MacKaye also produced a stream of articles and papers proposing innovative programs and approaches to regional planning such as "townless highways," "highwayless towns," a "Nature Guide Service," proposals for wilderness protection legislation, a "Bay Circuit" of 125,000 acres of protected land and water around Boston, and "wilderness ways" in Massachusetts and New Hampshire.

During a brief stint in South Dakota with the forerunner of the U.S. Bureau of Indian Affairs, MacKaye met Bob Marshall, the head of that agency's forestry division as well as noted author and conservationist Aldo Leopold. These meetings led to important personal and professional collaborations. MacKaye joined the Tennessee Valley Authority (TVA) as a "Regional Planner" in Knoxville and in that same year wrote the "Invitation to Help Organize a Group to Preserve the American Wilderness,"[7] which led directly to the formation of The Wilderness Society in 1935 with MacKaye as one of its founding leaders.

MacKaye ended his professional career with the U.S. Forest Service, which he had rejoined in 1937, before moving on to the Rural Electrification Administration in 1942. He retired from that assignment on his 66th birthday in 1945. The end of MacKaye's professional employment, however, was not the end of his career. In 1945, he began a 5-year term as president of The Wilderness Society, drafted federal wilderness legislation, and proposed a national system of "wilderness belts." At the completion of his term as president of The Wilderness Society, MacKaye became its honorary president and remained in that role for the rest of his life.

In 1954, MacKaye worked with Supreme Court Chief Justice William O. Douglas on a widely publicized walk-through of the C&O Canal, which helped save its long corridor from becoming another roadbed into Washington, DC. He won a number of awards including the annual conservation award from the Trustees of Reservations in 1954 and the U.S. Department of Interior Conservation Award in 1966. Even after his eyesight began to fail in the mid 1960s, MacKaye remained productive. He finished work on his major opus, *Geotechnics of North America,*[8] a 15-year effort that went unpublished. He also published a collection of his articles in *From Geography to Geotechnics,*[9] followed by his final retrospective book, *Expedition Nine: A Return to a Region*[10] in 1969.

Blind, in failing health, and cared for by a kind neighbor, in his final years MacKaye "held court" at his beloved "Cottage" in Shirley Center, where he received a steady stream of visitors and admirers, many of whom were from the Appalachian Trail community. Benton MacKaye passed away quietly and peacefully at home in 1975 at the age of 96.

Progressive Activist

The Progressive Era in the United States stretched roughly from the 1890s through the 1920s and sought mainly to bring efficiency and justice to society through the application of the best scientific practices available. As noted at the beginning of this text, it was an era of optimism among its proponents, especially those in government service, who felt they could make the world a better place through careful planning and benevolent government programs. MacKaye, frequently holding controversial political and social positions, was a progressive activist who stridently sought to advance progressive causes throughout the heyday of that period. In the 1910s and early 1920s he and his small group of like-minded "Hell Raisers" dubbed their Washington, DC home "Hell House" (probably as a play on the name of Jane Addams' "Hull House") and used it as their base of operations for political activism. Their efforts extended beyond the scope of their professional jobs and seemed to pervade much of their lives ranging from their official duties developing policies for their respective agencies, to deep discussions at "Hell House," to "suffragette hikes" MacKaye and others led around Washington on weekends. He and the other "Hell Raisers" were examples of what have been called "independent progressives."[11]

Benton MacKaye was nurtured by the leaders of the Progressive Era and played a significant role in furthering its ideals. His early positions with the newly created federal land management agencies placed him at the center of things. He worked with some of its most influential leaders including the Forest Service's Gifford Pinchot. MacKaye generated a series of creative and bold schemes, which nearly always carried the common thread of attempting to improve people's lives through the development and stewardship of natural resources, especially forest resources. This human focus made him a different kind of conservationist than his contemporaries. What is striking is how idealistic and brash he and his colleagues were. This was partly an outgrowth of being in the thick of federal service during the Progressive Era, but it was also a natural outgrowth of the "MacKaye Inheritance" and his lifelong personal convictions born of wide experience.

MacKaye's strong belief in the importance of community was shaped from growing up in idyllic Shirley Center, Massachusetts, as well as from observing the frequent absence of community in his work with the U.S. Forest Service. For example, one of the central problems he noted at an experimental government-planned community for World War I veterans was the isolation of families that he attributed to people picking their own parcels along the rail line rather than the government helping create a central community for them.

Trailblazer–The Appalachian Trail

The Appalachian Trail is a 2,175 mile footpath from Maine to Georgia. It is in all likelihood the most famous and well-known trail in the world. It is an icon, "one of the fine imaginative works of our generation,"[12] according to the urban and regional planner Lewis Mumford, and it was Benton MacKaye's idea. The Appalachian Trail that exists today, however, is only a small part of MacKaye's original vision.

Stories conflict about when and how Benton MacKaye first conceived of a very long "through trail" along the spine of the Appalachians. The most common recounting is that he first thought of the idea in 1912 while standing among the high peaks of Vermont. Other trail advocates at the time were talking about lengthening existing trails in New England, but no one had thought of anything even remotely as bold as what MacKaye was to propose.

MacKaye never envisioned the Appalachian Trail primarily as a trail. He imagined a wide and continuous belt of protected wilderness to serve as a "dam" against the "metropolitan invasion" he saw surging westward from eastern cities. He wanted the Appalachian Trail to be "a retreat from profit" that could give people a large, wild respite from their fast-paced lives and from the "wayside fungus" of commercial development. The Appalachian Trail was only one unifying aspect of his overall plan, which included a series of permanent communities, shelters, and food and farm camps where people could work together in common cause.

These notions were outgrowths of his earlier progressive plans to use the natural resources available on public lands as the basis for small communities that would better provide for the social and material needs of people. He was rebelling against the prevailing system that was dominated by large corporations that had little interest in sustainable resource use or the welfare of families. To MacKaye, the Appalachian Trail was going to be a means to an end. He was a dedicated hiker, to be sure, but in many respects his proposal for the longest trail ever conceived was a strategy to engage the outdoor recreation community in his more grandiose vision of managing landscapes and natural resources on a large scale to benefit society.

MacKaye was more than a competent forester, conservationist, and recreation advocate. His bigger objective was to:

> ...as far as practicable conserve the whole stretch of the
> Appalachians for recreation...Recreation in the biggest
> sense—the re-creation of the spirit that is being crushed by
> the machinery of the modern industrial city—the spirit of fel-
> lowship and cooperation...It is a plan for the conservation not
> of things—machines and land—but of men and their love of
> freedom and fellowship.[13]

MacKaye saw his Appalachian Trail proposal as a "flank attack" on "ultra conservatives" who would likely oppose his greater purpose – "an indirect route to his conception of the ideal American society."[14] He never retreated from these grander objectives for the Appalachian Trail, although nearly all who followed him took a much narrower view.

MacKaye and his key allies (many from his Regional Planning Association of America) began to use their professional and personal connections to expertly promote the broader idea of an Appalachian Trail. He was not just a dreamer as some would later disparagingly view him. He was strategic and focused on making his grand idea a reality. The initial mailing list he used to promote the idea for the trail included Gifford Pinchot and Jane Addams, among many other progressives and reformers. He wrote well-placed articles in major newspapers and magazines and spoke widely at meetings and other gatherings. His conviction was that the Appalachian Trail should be a decentralized effort, and his effective "evangelism" among trail advocates inspired many to action. He admonished an early gathering of Appalachian Trail leaders to, "walk softly and carry a big map." In creating the Appalachian Trail Conference in 1925, he and other key leaders sought to foster grassroots activism up and down the eastern seaboard that would be necessary to create and care for the Appalachian Trail. Correspondence from those early years contains references to MacKaye as "Nestor," a reference to the wise counselor in ancient Greek literature.[15]

Gradually, MacKaye's larger vision for the Appalachian Trail began to be overshadowed by the more limited, but still daunting, objective of building a 2,000 mile continuous trail for recreation. Conflicting philosophies became most apparent in MacKaye's interactions with the man most directly responsible for actually completing the Appalachian Trail, Myron Avery. Avery was an extraordinary leader and hard-driving lawyer who became involved in the volunteer effort when work on the project had begun to stall. Without Avery, the Appalachian Trail likely never would have been completed. He formed and served as the first president of the Potomac Appalachian Trail Club, a club that played a pivotal role in completing the trail. He scouted trail locations, organized other Appalachian Trail clubs, recruited countless volunteers, and wrote construction manuals and guidebooks. He was elected chairman of the overall Appalachian Trail Conference in 1931 and served in that role for the next 21 years. He was everything MacKaye was not; a pragmatic, get your hands dirty, finish the trail at all costs leader, who was called by some a "practical idealist." Avery was at odds with MacKaye, who saw the trail as a means to a larger end.

The catalyst for the biggest conflict between MacKaye and Avery was the proposal for Skyline Drive, a federal Depression era project to create a scenic mountain road in Virginia. The proposed route would obliterate large parts of the Appalachian Trail. Even more problematic for MacKaye and his allies was that it and similar mountain road proposals to follow (e.g., the Blue Ridge Parkway) would literally cut the remaining eastern wilderness in half. MacKaye felt that protecting the integrity of the wilderness corridor was at the heart of the purpose for creating the Appalachian Trail and that the Skyline Drive had to be stopped. He considered the "skyline drive" to be the "arch intruder" of the mountains and wilderness and proposed "flank roads" as a reasonable and far less destructive alternative. Avery argued that they did not have the political clout to fight the road, that the impact on the footpath itself would be minimal, and that impacts could be handled with the help of the Civilian Conservation Corps by simply relocating the affected segments. The conflict between the two came to a head at the 1935 meeting of the Appalachian Trail Conference, where Avery and his allies prevailed after a heated verbal battle.

Shortly thereafter, MacKaye and Avery severed their working relationship and MacKaye ended his association with the Appalachian Trail until after Avery's death in 1952. MacKaye felt the Appalachian Trail Conference had so diluted the purpose of the Appalachian Trail that he needed to work by other means to realize his more expansive vision. In retrospect, most observers believe that the estrangement between MacKaye and Avery was largely due to "radical differences in personal styles, strategy, and tactics, and fundamentally different philosophical concepts of what the Trail should be and become."[16]

Although the idea of a 2,000 mile footpath did prove to be compelling for Myron Avery and hundreds of equally dedicated volunteers (many of whom MacKaye recruited and inspired), the "wayside fungus" of commercial development in the 1950s and 1960s threatened the continuous route of the trail, which was frequently on private land. Vigorous lobbying by the Appalachian Trail Conference and many other conservation organizations and individuals led to the National Trails System Act of 1968 and its 1978 amendments. These actions authorized and funded the purchase of a protective corridor of land enveloping the Appalachian Trail. The Appalachian Trail Conference and the National Park Service formed a unique partnership that now protects a core of wild land surrounding the trail. Further efforts by the Appalachian Trail Conference, now called the Appalachian Trail Conservancy, are beginning to give new life to the broader Appalachian Trail corridor that MacKaye originally envisioned. He would, no doubt, be pleased by these efforts.

Without the completion of a "simple footpath" and the broad public support the trail itself engendered, a trail to serve as the backbone for the corridor MacKaye wanted would not have existed. MacKaye and Avery were both right, and there would likely be no Appalachian Trail at all today if both had not done what they did. More importantly, MacKaye's creativity and advice to "carry a big map" helped spawn other trails like the Appalachian Trail. Many of these initiatives would have pleased him since, "In MacKaye's thought the Appalachian Trail was only a baseline for a network of cooperatively organized spurs and trails that would some day cover the earth."[17]

A Father of the Wilderness Movement

The preservation of a vast wild area in the Appalachian Mountains was a central part of Benton MacKaye's original purpose in proposing the Appalachian Trail. As he said to the Appalachian Trail leadership in 1935:

> The physical path is no end in itself; it is a means of sojourning in the primeval or wilderness environment whose preservation and nurture is your particular care...The Appalachian Trail as originally conceived is not merely a footpath *through* the wilderness but a footpath *of* the wilderness...the Appalachian Trail is a wilderness trail or it is nothing.[18]

As mentioned, MacKaye ceased active involvement with the Appalachian Trail effort because he felt its other leaders no longer shared his vision. He refocused his efforts more directly on wilderness preservation itself. The direct impact of carving mountain roads like the Skyline Drive through the heart of the remaining wild country in the eastern United States played a big part in his decision to refine his strategy for wilderness protection. MacKaye anticipated the devastating impact roads could have on wilderness. Equally disturbing was that the National Park Service, the agency MacKaye felt should be most diligent in protecting the remaining wilderness, was the agency advocating and building the mountain roads he abhorred. The urgency of these issues prompted him to action. As he saw it, "This clash of 'Trail vs. Highway' on the mountain tops is something bigger than it seems. It is an early skirmish, perhaps the first significant skirmish, in the retention of a humanly balanced world. This is the world that the Wilderness Society was formed to fight for."[19]

MacKaye and other wilderness advocates were coming to the same conclusion. A new and independent organization that was unequivocally pro-wilderness was needed. MacKaye met with his like-minded acquaintances Bob Marshall and Harold Anderson in Knoxville, Tennessee, where they expanded Anderson's idea for an anti-skyline road group into a national wilderness advocacy organization. MacKaye then drafted his "Invitation to Help Organize a Group to Preserve the American Wilderness."

After revisions, MacKaye, Marshall, Harvey Broome, and Bernard Frank signed it and mailed copies to a small hand-picked group of influential people including Aldo Leopold, John Collier, John Merriam, and Robert Sterling Yard. The invitation included the exhortation, "...the time has come, with the brutalizing pressure of a spreading metropolitan civilization, to recognize this wilderness environment as a serious need rather than a luxury and a plaything."[20] MacKaye and Marshall became the driving forces on an eight-person organizing committee.

The Wilderness Society was formally incorporated in 1937. MacKaye became its first vice president with Yard as president and Marshall's brother George added to the leadership council. They pulled together a team of conservation luminaries to advance the wilderness protection agenda. Unfortunately, Bob Marshall died suddenly in 1939. However, the Robert Marshall Wilderness Fund established with part of his personal fortune provided support for The Wilderness Society's efforts. The group's influence increased and MacKaye was an important principal, writing frequently for the organization's main publication, *Living Wilderness,* and providing inspiration and leadership on many fronts.

In retrospect, MacKaye's wilderness advocacy was nuanced. He was not a simple or predictable preservationist, for whom protection of wild areas for its own sake was the ultimate objective. "He never thought of the wilderness as the last refuge of despairing hermits…He was never a mere simple-lifer, still less an anti-urbanist."[21] He "moved humanity back to the center of the stage and relegated technology to a supporting role, but he did not banish it. He was not a Luddite; he only sought balance between means and ends."[22]

Regional Planning and Geotechnics

MacKaye was a planner no matter the project, but always "in the high strategic sense: one who, in his own words, carefully works out Plans A, B, and C, thinking he has provided for every contingency, and then, when the situation turns out different, throws them aside and improvises Plan F. Plan F, MacKaye knew, would not be possible if much work had not gone into A, B, and C."[23] Unlike many environmentalists, however, MacKaye's planning was motivated by more than simply a concern for the natural world. His primary concern was people, their communities, and society in general. He used conservation strategies in general and regional planning in particular as tools to accomplish what were ultimately social reforms.

MacKaye described his work as "geotechnics," which he defined as "the applied science of making the earth more habitable."[24] He pursued that work with remarkable zeal. "For MacKaye, environmental quality was not a legalistic exercise of minimizing air, water, and noise pollution, but the creation and conservation of the environment that would allow the greatest development of the human potential, whether urban, rural, or wilderness."[25]

When he spoke of geotechnics as being concerned with "habitability," MacKaye always intended to entail a balance among what he felt were three components – physical, economic, and social habitability. To him, achieving such a balance required maintaining ecological health (physical), assuring an area would enable men and women to make a living (economic), and enabling people to enjoy living (social). He felt that people who worked to make the earth "more habitable" entered either through "Gate 1" (the physical approach) or "Gate 2" (the social approach) and saw his geotechnics as necessary to effectively marry the two. He has been accurately described as what we would now refer to as an "ecological humanist," whose work focused on the influence of the environment on the spirit of man.[26] He worked from an underlying Emersonian belief in the importance of harmony between society and Nature. The environment was the source from which a genuine culture grew.[27]

MacKaye's planning work throughout his long and productive career advanced a number of interrelated themes. One was his uncommonly broad and integrated planning perspective. He was ahead of his times by treating landscapes on a regional scale, and he was an early proponent of considering watersheds (or at least river valleys) as essential planning elements. He called the watershed the "geotechnic unit." Even before aerial photography and more advanced forms of remote sensing, he seemed to naturally adopt the "planetary feeling" he often wrote about. He envisioned landscapes and entire regions from an appropriately broad and integrated perspective. His underlying planning philosophy of considering the interrelationship of environmental and human needs on large (often grand) scales, was apparent in his work with progressive era federal agencies, in his efforts on behalf of the Regional Planning Association of America, and in his wide ranging planning and policy proposals.

A second recurring theme in MacKaye's planning was his focus on developing and nurturing healthy communities. In many respects, his native town of Shirley Center and the human and natural landscapes that surrounded it became the pattern for others he tried to nurture and preserve. He noted, "The community *par excellence* was (and is) the New England village,"[28] arranged around a publicly owned "commons" or "folkland," belonging to the whole community. He felt that the "move-on" culture of the pioneers was one of the reasons that people were often unconcerned about conserving their communities and other special places and resources. In many of his proposals, he sought to counteract this destructive tendency. In a similar way, he also saw private land ownership taken to its extreme as a significant societal problem since individuals could then use land and other resources any way they chose without regard for others in or around their communities. Consequently, MacKaye was an outspoken opponent of outdated homestead laws and other efforts to transfer lands out of public ownership. "He hated, down to the depth of his soul, all despoilers of the land,"[29] in part, because of the negative effects on communities and their residents.

He considered uncontrolled highway development a particularly destructive threat to the healthy communities he sought to foster, and he had a firm belief that highways were actually powerful "region-makers." This was the root of his increasing concern about the "wayside fungus" of commercial development and what he called "motor slums" (a term he credited to Walter Prichard Eaton) which grew along highways. He felt these were grave threats to preserving a "proper balance between urban, rural, and primeval environments." Consequently, he advocated policies and actions that would lead to distinct communities separated from through roads and surrounded by undeveloped areas that would help them maintain their "individuality" rather than policies that would eventually lead to "one endless roadtown." In today's vernacular we would say that he was concerned about preserving a region's distinctiveness and "sense of place." For example, he proposed systems of "dams" (e.g., the Appalachian Trail corridor) and "levees" of protected public lands ("townless highway" corridors) to hem in this relentless "invasion" of metropolitan growth. He compared modern cities to glaciers, "spreading, unthinking, ruthless" that "submerge" and "iron away" the distinctiveness and "personality" of the existing communities in the path of their "metropolitan invasion" and worked steadily to direct and contain their destructive spread. All these proposals were ways of managing development and "flows" so that people could enjoy the benefits of small "indigenous" towns and wild lands where they could escape and drink deeply of the rejuvenating elixir of nature.

Another common planning theme for MacKaye was embodied in his sometimes rambling ideas about "outdoor culture," which he regarded as "the soul and body of regional planning." He felt outdoor culture involved "a special kind of ability: the ability to visualize a happier state of affairs than the average humdrum of the regulation world," and through it was trying to help people recognize the possibility of "a new mode of life." A key element was the harmony and balance of a pleasing environment that would help counter the tendency for society to "overcivilize." The main threat to advancing outdoor culture, according to MacKaye, was the modern metropolis:

> Less and less is it indigenous; more and more is it a standardized exotic…It depends on tentacles rather than on roots…an unbalanced industrial life…is the cause of an unbalanced recreational life. For its hectic influence widens the breach between normal work and play by segmenting the worst elements in each…[30]

It is striking that MacKaye made such observations about urbanization, work, and play at a time when the environment was far more balanced than it is today, and decades before television and the Internet have driven the lives of most people even farther from what he would have considered a healthy embodiment of outdoor culture.

MacKaye's outdoor culture philosophy is best captured in his 1929 article "Outdoor Culture—The Philosophy of Through Trails."[31] He metaphorically suggests that overcivilized ancient Rome could be considered fortunate that it was overrun by barbarians since they brought a "cleansing" invasion from the hinterland. American civilization had not yet received a modern counterpart that could help it better embrace outdoor culture. He proposed that such a cleansing of overcivilization could come, in part, as a result of long distance "through trails" and the modern nature-loving "barbarians" who would use them. They could come back from experiences in places like the Appalachian Trail and spread their "outdoor culture" back to the rest of society. His utopian outdoor culture philosophy was rooted in restoring the harmony and balance of the "indigenous environment" into our mode of living. "This philosophy—or culture—is, to my mind, the *raison d'etre* of the through trail and its ramifications. It is 'the why' of the Appalachian Trail, which—let us hope—may some day form the base for the strategy of a 'Barbarian invasion,' and for the development of a Barbarian Utopia."[32]

As early as the 1920s, MacKaye pointed out that early settlers created "inroads of population through the forest," but that, "to restore civilization," we "must develop forest inroads between our population centers." He saw these forest inroads as a sound basis for a recreation plan and that they "should form a series of embankments, or 'levees,' for controlling the flood of mechanistic civilization which is pouring forth..." As modern greenway planners suggest, he proposed that these should follow mountain ranges, river valleys, etc. and that they could be called "wilderness ways." "They should form a network of public parks and forests connected by a series of paths or primitive trails equipped with cabins and facilities for camping and general outdoor living." He felt the real basis for developing "the proper setting and environment for the activity of outdoor recreation and of the pursuit of culture at its sources, is more than physical—it is psychologic. It consists in the creation or development of a genuine human interest..." He optimistically saw this tendency in the American outdoor movement of the time and felt it was an "inevitable and irresistible impulse of humanity to right the balance of its civilization." His concern about human welfare and how the forces of progress in general, and changes in the landscape in particular, affected the common good, infused his planning philosophy. Planning ideas similar to those promoted by MacKaye generations ago are alive and well today, although few of their proponents have ever heard of him.

Independent Scholar and Mentor

Although MacKaye had a long and varied professional career, his work can best be described as that of an independent scholar. Above all, he was an intellectual and a philosopher who had an uncanny knack for looking into the future and conceiving of ways to shape it, generally by using conservation as a tool to achieve multiple ends. One approach he used particularly effectively was investing his time and talents in others and serving as a mentor to them.

He had many friends but valued his solitude and quiet, especially in the upstairs "Sky Parlor" of his family "Cottage" in Shirley Center, where he wrote and read during his career and particularly after his retirement in 1945. Much of his life was centered on reading, writing, and discourse with friends and colleagues. One of his close friends said, "One is impressed by the amount of reading done by this outdoorsman. But the most lingering impression is that of a highly original and creative mind."[33] Although he was a university faculty member for only a short time at Harvard, he was a scholar in the broadest and most meaningful sense. He wrote at least 60 articles in magazines and journals and penned essays and other publications as well.

Writing was a powerful tool that MacKaye cultivated and used effectively. His father had known both Emerson and Thoreau:

> ...and had given his family's life an air...of high serious-
> ness...Young Benton early reacted against the mercurial
> impracticality of his idealistic father, but he absorbed his
> father's vision of improving human society. The result for
> Benton was an Emersonian idealism grounded in a Thoreau-
> vian appreciation of practical ways and means. In this con-
> text, writing became for Benton an essential tool, first to
> organize his ideas, then to explain, to persuade and to teach.[34]

MacKaye wrote about the natural world because of his concern for humanity. He was not a "nature writer" in the popular sense of the term.[35]

MacKaye's intellectual perspective was far broader than the vast majority of his contemporaries. It was global, with his ultimate focus directed toward a "habitable globe." From this perspective, for example, he suggested Antarctica be made the first public domain of the United Nations. From this planetary viewpoint he admonished, "Global environment—this 'one thing in common' —the sense of it, what I call 'terrestrial consciousness'—that, I submit, is the starting point of the way of ways to global order."[36] He called on us "to enlarge the understanding of natural processes" through firsthand experiences interacting with nature. He felt that interacting with nature was one of the most important functions of wilderness areas and national parks worldwide.

In reading MacKaye's writings and reading about him from the perspectives of his closest friends and colleagues, we are struck by the powerful and productive impressions he made on others. He inspired them, served as a trusted and valued mentor, and was a teacher in the broadest sense of the term. As one of them observed, he "...never tried to be the expert seeking to impose a plan upon the layman. Rather, he tried to inform the layman and persuade him to join in his vision."[37] During his years with the Tennessee Valley Authority, his "...greatest tour de force...was his influence on other people and their ideas…about once a week…he would pep up others with his fresh ideas and imagination and then disappear upstairs again."[38] "He liked good talk with his friends, a 'bully pow-wow'…" but "Always his questioning banter would bring a conversation around to serious matters."[39] He "radiated on behalf of agency and region the same enthusiasm for goals and expectations that had inspired the first organizational steps for the Appalachian Trail a decade earlier."[40]

One of the best examples of his approach to nurturing his visions and passing them on to others were the gatherings he organized with friends and protégés while working in Knoxville. They were known as "The Philosophers' Club." Through Benton's leadership and love of life, this group met regularly for chats at Benton's apartment, hiked, read, and danced together. His friends and associates remembered their interactions with him fondly, but these associations also proved to be an effective means for refining and spreading his innovative ideas.

His informal "Philosophers' Club" also illustrates how he seamlessly mixed his professional and personal life in serving as an effective mentor. This approach was also seen in his interactions with students on and off campus while a faculty member at Harvard, in the schemes hatched at "Hell House," and during his early "suffragette hikes" outside Washington, DC. He had a "warm and generous spirit" that was widely known and a personality that served "as a catalytic agent, bringing about reactions in those his mind touches…"[41] This was certainly the case during his long involvement with the Wilderness Society that his friends and colleagues remembered so fondly. "His breadth of experience in land-use planning and his great ability to inspire others in the fields of his interest were invaluable throughout all those early years of the Society."[42]

An Unconventional Life

MacKaye had non-traditional priorities throughout his life. He never strived for fame or fortune nor sought center stage for himself, although he was tenacious in promoting his many grand ideas. His biographer calls MacKaye's a "resolutely unconventional American life, which was zestfully pursued on a plane of extraordinary idealism, hope, and vision."[43] According to his close friend Lewis Mumford, "He lives a very quiet and abstemious life: plain living and high thinking; and wastes less of his time on the means of living than anyone I know."[44] MacKaye once joked that his primary source of income was not having children. Throughout his life he consciously lived by a maxim that he and his brother shared, "simple tastes are better than any others."[45] After MacKaye's death, his closest collaborator, Mumford, said of him, "Though he was so different a character from Thoreau, he figures for me as Thoreau's latest continuator…"[46]

One of the roots of MacKaye's unconventional philosophy was a concern for people's leisure and recreation. He was convinced that in the future people would work less and have more leisure and that leisure was essential. "The less time spent in drudging to secure the means for mere existence, the more time we have left to use these means for actual living."[47] He said further:

> Recreation is not necessary for bodily existence (except for a certain minimum), but it *is* necessary for real living. Recreation is not merely 'non-industry,' it is the reason for industry. Industry provides existence which is the base for living. Recreation is incipient culture—the final lap in the pursuit of happiness. Its objectives are not finite, they are infinite. They are the mysteries and the melodies of creation...."[48]

Even more characteristic of his life's work, however, was his contention that a balanced environment would be essential for a culture with more leisure and that conserving such an environment would be critical for the future.

Much of MacKaye's lifestyle embodied the classical notion of pure leisure. He had almost no concern for money, and he felt that the pursuit of wealth was not a good objective or investment. Most of what he did was intrinsically motivated. Just as the ancient Greeks suggested that virtuous individuals could nurture a virtuous society, MacKaye's passionate efforts to advance what he and his siblings called their "greater work" did spill over to benefit society in lasting ways. The vast majority of his policy proposals throughout his career were ultimately directed toward the pursuit of happiness for the largest number of people. Not only did he advocate this philosophy, he lived it and lived it well.

Benton MacKaye's Legacy

In some ways Benton MacKaye's life and work had mixed results. He developed remarkably bold and grand ideas, but few were actually implemented. Even those that were, like the Appalachian Trail, ended up changed in ways that fell short of his original vision. No doubt, however, his ideas had profound effects. They reverberate in the grassroots trails and greenways movement, bioregionalism, New Urbanism, Neotraditionalism, conservation biology, landscape ecology, debates about the meaning of wilderness, ecological restoration, environmental justice, and civic environmentalism.[49] Some of his proposals are now being rediscovered, refined, and applied anew. He predicted many of the growth-related problems we face today and he proposed innovative solutions that deserve our attention.

Benton MacKaye lived a life of ideas and action. He created innovative plans for making the world a better place through his service living. More importantly, he had the personality and unflagging determination to inspire others to help transform his visions into reality. In his 1921 article proposing the Appalachian Trail, MacKaye asked readers to consider the perspective of a giant striding southward along the Appalachian ridges. He wanted to force the reader into a regional view of planning that encompassed wild lands, the not-too-distant urban areas, and everything in between. After making his observations and proposals, MacKaye concluded, "Such are the outlooks—such are the opportunities—seen by a discerning spirit from the Appalachian skyline."

From our vantage point more than four generations later, it is easy to see that Benton MacKaye was indeed a giant with a remarkably discerning spirit. He embodied service living in advocating for a perspective that was far reaching for its time. We remain the beneficiaries of his visionary thinking and effective calls to action.

V
Our Lady of the Glades: Marjory Stoneman Douglas and Florida's "River of Grass"

Everglade

An everglade might be defined most easily as a swampy tract covered with tall grass and dotted with occasional trees. In practice, however, the word almost always refers to the grand marsh of southern Florida, which is so flat that a broad sheet of water flows slowly across it on the way to the sea—a river with a valley so shallow it is measured in inches. The system is so finely balanced that minute variations in elevation can lead to dramatic changes in flora and fauna. The etymology of everglade is obscure, but "ever" may have been used to mean "interminable." If so, it was a misnomer, for changes in land use and irrigation north of the Everglades have altered the flow of water and driven the area's unique plants, animals, and processes to the point of extinction. As the twenty-first century begins, it is the site of the largest attempt at ecosystem restoration any place on the face of the globe, an expensive and desperate attempt to keep the concept of the everglade alive.[1]

—Bill McKibben

If we sainted people for their environmentalism, Marjory Stoneman Douglas would be near the top of most any list. As one of the 20th century's greatest environmental writers and activists, her achievements were Herculean. She brought national attention to the Everglades at a time when that watery region of South Florida was in greatest danger of drying up from a rapidly expanding, and largely unfeeling, human population bent on developing what was thought to be a worthless and unsightly "swamp."

What is most remarkable about the Marjory Stoneman Douglas story is the magnitude of her accomplishments given the constraints placed on women throughout much of the 20th century, and the unlikely set of circumstances that led her to be in the right place at the right time to make a monumental difference in the course of American environmental history. Her story stands as powerful testimony to the importance of conviction of purpose, perseverance, the unflagging nature of the human spirit, and the wisdom contained in the age-old adage that "it's never too late to get things done."

Whether we attribute Douglas' environmental contributions to providence, personality, or just plain luck, she was first and foremost a writer, and only secondarily an environmentalist. Although her groundbreaking 1947 book *The Everglades: River of Grass*[2] galvanized public opinion regarding the significance of the Everglades ecosystem and the threats posed to it, yet another 20 years would pass before she would roll up her sleeves and get down to work as an environmental activist. She was 78 at the time. A full accounting of her story thus demands taking the long view, a view befitting a woman who lived to the ripe old age of 108.

Inauspicious Beginnings

Long before her environmental accomplishments, a combination of forces shaped and molded Douglas' character. Born April 7, 1890 in Minneapolis, Minnesota to Frank Bryant Stoneman and Florence Lillian Trefethen, Marjory entered the world weighing a robust 12 pounds. Body image would become a lifelong issue for her. Whether she had an unduly critical view of her own appearance, or whether she was merely being realistic, the little girl did not think herself pretty. Years later she would write:

> Gold-rimmed glasses were the crowning unattractive feature
> on an unattractive child in general . . . . I was a fat little child
> and a fat little girl because in those days it was considered
> healthy to have fat children and I was plied with the best of
> butter, cream, pancakes, and everything fattening there was.
> To top it off, I had stringy, kind of mouse-colored hair.[3]

The Stoneman family moved to Providence, Rhode Island when Marjory was three. The circumstances surrounding the move were ominous. Frank Stoneman was reputed to have been involved in some questionable business practices in Minnesota, and that may have prompted the relocation. The problem repeated itself in Providence. When Marjory was five, her parents separated and her mother took her to live with her maternal grandparents in Taunton, Massachusetts. Her parents' separation weighed heavily on the little girl throughout her childhood, and a dysfunctional family life contributed to a lifelong skepticism and distrust of others. To make matters worse, not long after her father left the household, Marjory's mother suffered a nervous breakdown from which she never fully recovered.

Marjory took refuge in reading. She quickly graduated from magazines to books and discovered that book learning served her well in school. She also took elocution classes, favoring voice training over the piano lessons her grandmother foisted upon her. At the end of the 19th century, young women were typically limited to teaching school or giving music lessons, and Marjory's grandmother was trying to prepare her granddaughter as best she could for a practical career. But there was nothing practical about Marjory Stoneman. She was neither musically inclined nor interested in teaching.

Emboldened by her learning, Marjory became more and more expressive. As she remembered it, her first independent thought occurred when she realized Santa Claus could not possibly make it down all those chimneys the night before Christmas. She concluded that Santa Claus could not be real. Her family conceded the point. In time, Marjory would come to see herself as a "subjective extrovert,"[4] a little girl with an active outer life masking an equally active hidden inner life.

Rounding out her increasingly extroverted persona was a strong Quaker influence from her father's side of the family, an influence characterized by independent thinking and pigheadedness. Marjory delighted in those qualities. She reveled in stories about her great-great Uncle Levi Coffin, President of the Underground Railroad that served as a conduit for slaves trying to escape the South at the time of the Civil War. Indeed, Marjory's ancestors had abandoned North Carolina for Ohio and Indiana so they wouldn't have to raise their children in a slave-holding state. Marjory thought slavery an abomination, and she relished the idea that she was related to someone who had taken a leadership role in righting that ethical wrong.

Marjory first realized she had a writer's temperament in high school. Though not a particularly good student, she was a good researcher and she knew how to get to the facts. She also polished her prose and poetry, and upon the occasion of her high school graduation on June 12, 1908, her "Parting Ode" was published in the graduation program. The last stanza hints at her troubled past and the hope of better things to come:

We have climbed together in sunny weather,
And in days when the clouds were black,
So linger we here, with a smile and a tear,
To send our farewells back.
But the trail calls us on; let us turn and be gone,
For the heights are yet to be passed.
With courage to strive and with purpose alive
Let us climb bravely on to the last.[5]

Wellesley College

As her mother's mental condition deteriorated, Marjory's Aunt Fanny took on the role of principal caregiver, which included providing money for Marjory's college education. The family preferred that she choose a local college, but Marjory's heart was set on Wellesley College in Boston. Aunt Fanny made the necessary financial sacrifice, and Marjory was sent off for the first time in her life to experience the world on her own.

The young Miss Stoneman was conflicted about leaving her mother to attend Wellesley. She understood that she had been the center of her mother's existence, and that even though her mother wanted her to go to college, doing so would likely contribute to her mother's further demise. Marjory came home to visit frequently during those college years. She bore a sense of guilt for having left her mother, but she was also enjoying a newfound sense of freedom. Marjory also was aware that while she was away at college, the family's resources back in Taunton were stretched to the limit to make it possible for her to gain a higher education.

The Wellesley years were filled with new experiences, new friends, and new subject matters. Marjory sampled the curriculum taught by Wellesley's distinguished faculty including a course taught by Emily Greene Balch, the Nobel Prize-winning economist. Professor Balch made a particularly strong impression on Marjory by taking her and her privileged classmates out of the cloistered environs of Wellesley to witness the harsh realities of Boston's slums. The field trips stimulated Marjory's interest in the plight of the socially and economically disadvantaged, a theme that would surface again and again throughout her writing life.

Marjory also continued to perfect her writing and speaking skills. She took advantage of most everything Wellesley had to offer, including editing the college annual, *Legenda,* in her senior year, and playing Friar Tuck in *Sherwood Forest,* the senior play.[6] "As Wellesley developed young women's skills," she recalled years later, "they became more convinced of their right to use them."[7] Clearly, Wellesley had a liberating effect on Marjory Stoneman. She began to see her future in a brighter light.

Coincident with Marjory's graduation from Wellesley was the death of her mother. In addition to her mental illness, Florence had been diagnosed with breast cancer. In the months leading up to her passing, the cancer had metastasized and spread to her spine, and the family knew it was just a matter of time. They waited until after Marjory's graduation to give her the sad news. Marjory rushed home to be with her mother during her final days. In retrospect, Florence's passing was a blessing. Aunt Fanny understood from the outset that Marjory's presence in her mother's life was what kept her mother alive. For Marjory to have a chance at living her own life, however, she would have to distance herself from her mother. Death provided that opportunity.

An Ill-Fated Marriage

Marjory's well-educated Wellesley friends scattered across the country to embark on new careers while she stumbled half-heartedly into a variety of teaching-related positions with two department stores—Nugent's in St. Louis, Missouri and Bamberger's in Newark, New Jersey. Marjory did not find the work fulfilling. She had never wanted to be a teacher. She was, in her words, "just making a living."[8]

She was also lonely. Then, through an acquaintance, Marjory met Kenneth Douglas, a man 30 years her senior who took an interest in her. As she told the story, "We exchanged pleasantries, and as I started to walk away he spoke to me again. No man had ever spoken to me again."[9] Three months later they married.

Kenneth Douglas turned out to be a con man. After a whirlwind honeymoon at the Hotel Belmont in New York City where Marjory "discovered sex,"[10] she responded to a loud knock on her apartment door only to be told brusquely by a policeman that a warrant was out for her husband's arrest. Mrs. Douglas had been ensconced in a "nuptial trance,"[11] and now she was being brought back harshly to reality. She wanted to be loyal to her new husband, but it was evident he wasn't who he was portraying himself to be. She had married a criminal. Douglas was imprisoned for writing bad checks, and in anticipation of his release, Marjory's family admonished her to divorce him and move on.

Uncle Ned, a seldom seen brother to her long lost father, laid out the facts regarding Marjory's future prospects should she stay wed to Mr. Douglas. The upshot was that it was high time to divorce Douglas, move to Miami, and be reunited with her father—all at the urging of her father's new wife, Lilla.

Marjory's ill-fated marriage to Kenneth Douglas resulted in two conclusions that would influence the unfolding of the rest of her life. First, she realized that in trying to be a good wife, she had allowed Kenneth to dominate her. She vowed never again to give herself over to the control or even the slightest possible domination of anybody, particularly a man.[12] Second, she wrote off sex. "Without the experience of marriage," she said, "brief though it turned out to be, I wouldn't have been able to meet the rest of my life with the balance which I seem to have been able to attain. In other words, I got sex out of the way."[13]

The Miami Herald

Marjory reunited with her estranged father at the train station in Miami. His reaction to seeing her after so many years was anything but reassuring.

> He expected a pretty girl, but now I wasn't. My face was always a bit crooked, and if anything it had become crookeder. That's why he took a good look at me and then started to back up—a slight and almost imperceptible jerk backward. He couldn't help it. My mother was beautiful.[14]

Whatever misgivings Marjory had about the reunion were quickly dispelled by Frank's wife, Lilla. She greeted Marjory with warmth and enthusiasm. Marjory soon learned that Lilla and Frank had been friends for years, and that they had waited two years after the death of Marjory's mother to get married. Frank filled his daughter in on his life. After his separation from her mother, he studied law, passed the bar, and moved to Orlando to practice. He met and fell in love with Lilla, but would not marry her since he had not divorced Marjory's mother. He went on to insist that it was Florence who had deserted him, and that he had been ostracized by her side of the family. After a decade struggling as an attorney in Orlando, he secured an old flatbed press as payment on a debt and moved to Miami to start its first morning paper, the *News Record*. In 1910 he reconfigured it as *The Miami Herald*.

In these "getting to know you" talks with her father, Marjory first learned about the plight of the Everglades. Florida's governor at the time, Napoleon Bonaparte Broward, was encouraging the rapid development of South Florida, which required dredging the "swamp." Through his position as editor of *The Miami Herald*, Frank Stoneman was one of the few people who stood up to the governor and questioned the logic of uncontrolled growth. The year was 1915.

It didn't take Marjory long to land a job on her father's newspaper. Asked to fill in temporarily for the society editor, she soon took over full-time. What she wrote didn't matter. She was ecstatic to be writing and getting paid for it. The editorial position also served as an entrée into Miami's social and political life. She befriended the wife of William Jennings Bryan, the renowned orator who took on Clarence Darrow in the Scopes trial. A devoted suffragist, Mrs. Bryan quickly drew Marjory into the suffrage movement, culminating in her testifying on behalf of a Florida Suffrage Amendment before a subcommittee of the Florida legislature. Though her elocution training served her well, her testimony fell on deaf ears. "Talking to them was like talking to graven images," she sighed. "They never paid any attention to us at all. They weren't even listening."[15] Such was Douglas' introduction to Florida politics. She learned that North Florida controlled the legislature, and the legislature behaved as if there were no South Florida.

In the summer of 1916, Marjory allowed herself to fall in love again. Cupid couldn't have struck at a worse time. World War I was in full force and her beau enlisted in the American Ambulance Service. He was soon shipped overseas to France. Following in his footsteps, Marjory joined the Navy and then transferred to the Red Cross. She ended up in Paris, but the relationship she sought never had a chance to materialize, and her new-found love came home a veteran changed by the war. Though Douglas maintained several close male friendships throughout the rest of her life, none would blossom into a full-fledged romance. As she summed up this aspect of her life, "I was beginning to realize that I was not the marrying kind. In my secret heart, I didn't want to get married again. I never wanted children. I wanted books."[16] From that time onward, Douglas sublimated any feelings she might have had about men, sex, and marriage into a higher calling—writing.

An Emerging Regional Writer

After the First World War, Marjory resumed her work on *The Miami Herald*. She wrote a column called "The Galley" and went about the business of immersing herself in South Florida issues. Her progressive leanings were evident as she railed against various social injustices accompanying Miami's rapid growth. She took a special interest in public health and child welfare, and she challenged the city to take action in righting the wrongs she brought to her readership's attention. During this period, Douglas met David Fairchild, an entomologist who would someday establish what is known today as Fairchild Tropical Gardens. Fairchild stimulated Douglas' interest in the flora and fauna of South Florida, and that in turn stimulated her interest in wanting to know more about the Everglades.

Douglas wrote about most anything that caught her fancy, and she developed the habit of inserting poetry into her column. One of her noteworthy poems concerned the fate of a young North Dakota man named Martin Tabert who had wandered into Florida, only to be arrested by the authorities as a vagrant. He was confined to a labor camp and beaten to death. As this last stanza from "Martin Tabert of North Dakota" illustrates, her poetry was haunting, and it was written to stir Florida's citizens to action:

The whip is still in the convict camps, for Florida's
    stirring now.
Children, from Key West to Pensacola you can hear the
    great wind go.
The wind that he roused when he lay dying,
The angry voice of Florida crying,
"Martin Tabert of North Dakota,
Martin Tabert of North Dakota,
Martin Tabert of North Dakota.
You can rest from your walking now!"[17]

The poem had a profound impact on Floridians and served as a catalyst for legislative reform that improved the way labor camp inmates were treated. Douglas was proud of her role in helping change the law. She felt she had finally made a difference with her writing.

Marjory continued to focus on South Florida matters, and it became increasingly apparent to her readers that she was developing into an important regional writer. Much of what she wrote centered on the geography, landscape, and people of South Florida, including periodic stories about the Everglades. However, her strong Op-Ed style frequently put her at odds with her father's point of view as well as that of *The Miami Herald*'s publisher. Her bosses were particularly displeased with her drawing attention to Miami's squalor and poverty. They would have preferred that she focus her writing on the positive aspects of Miami's growth and development. The friction took its toll on Marjory's health and she suffered a nervous breakdown in 1924. Her doctor recommended that she resign from the *Herald* for health reasons. Welcoming the prescription, she quickly followed his advice.

Freed from the pressure of constant deadlines, Marjory honed her craft as a short story writer. Throughout the 1920s and 1930s, she contributed a stream of stories to *The Saturday Evening Post*. Among them were "A Bird Dog in the Hand,"[18] about the tension between development interests in South Florida and associated threats to the Everglades; "Wings,"[19] about the killing of South Florida's water birds for their decorative feathers; "September-Remember,"[20] about the devastation brought about by hurricanes in South Florida; and "The Road to the Horizon,"[21] anticipating the building of the Tamiami Trail across the Everglades in 1928. With the publication of these stories, and a readership in the millions, Douglas' reputation grew and she prospered as a freelance writer. At the height of her short story career, she was fetching $1,200 per story,[22] which was a significant amount of money, especially during the Depression years.

With proceeds from *The Saturday Evening Post* stories, Marjory built a small bungalow in Coconut Grove, a quaint, garden-like community on the south side of Miami. The bungalow was set back from the street and did not include a driveway. Douglas didn't own a car, didn't care to drive one, and would never bother to learn. The bungalow itself was sparsely furnished. It satisfied the needs of a writer and her closest companions—cats and books.

Marjory learned more and more about the Everglades. She befriended a landscape architect named Ernest Coe who was spearheading an initiative to create Everglades National Park. For several years she served on Coe's advisory committee. She also visited the Everglades occasionally, though she was quick to point out that her interest in them was more intellectual than anything else.

> To be a friend of the Everglades is not necessarily to spend time wandering around out there. It's too buggy, too wet, too generally inhospitable for camping or hiking or the other outdoors activities which naturalists in other places can routinely enjoy. When newspeople come down and say, "Let's go out in the Everglades, just like you always do," I often laugh. I hardly ever go into the Everglades.[23]

The Everglades had two seasons, she teased, mosquito and non-mosquito. Her concern for the glades was also influenced by their significance to the regionalism now flavoring many of her short stories.

In 1938, Marjory lost her Aunt Fanny in Taunton, and in 1941 her father, Frank, in Miami. Their deaths removed the lifelong schism Marjory had felt between her northern and southern selves. No longer divided, she believed she was finally a complete being. "It was the end of my immature life, if one can say that at the age of 51, and the beginning of a new maturity."[24]

The Everglades: River of Grass

Soon thereafter, Hervey Allen, author of the best-selling *Anthony Adverse*,[25] dropped by Coconut Grove for a visit. His publisher, Rinehart and Company, had appointed him editor of its Rivers of America series as a reward for his own writing success. He was interested in recruiting Douglas to write a book about the Miami River. She pointed out that it would have to be a short book, because the Miami River was only one mile long. She wondered whether the story might be connected to the larger Everglades somehow, and asked Allen if he would consider a broader definition of what constituted a river. He was agreeable and advanced Marjory $1,000 to begin work.

Douglas immediately sought the assistance of *The Miami Herald*'s new editor, John Pennekamp. He sent her to Garald Parker, the state hydrologist. Parker read her the official definition of a river, and they both decided the Everglades could indeed be construed of as a "river of grass." In a few years those three simple words would come to define the meaning of the ecosystem known as the Everglades for the entire world.

It took Douglas five years to write *The Everglades: River of Grass*. Its publication in November, 1947, coincided with the realization of Ernest Coe's dream, the establishment of Everglades National Park. Marjory attended the dedication ceremony in Everglades City, Florida on December 6th, though for some reason she declined to take center stage with President Harry Truman, Coe, and other dignitaries. She then witnessed her book rise to the ranks of an internationally acclaimed best-seller. She had, for the second time in her life, made a significant difference with her writing.

In retrospect, the genius of *The Everglades: River of Grass* was in Douglas' portrayal of the Everglades as an ecosystem, a highly intricate and interconnected web of life that depends on an uninterrupted flow of water from Central to Southern Florida. In the book's opening paragraph, she introduces the Everglades in a way that makes us begin to care about what we might otherwise easily dismiss as an unsightly, uninviting, and unimportant swamp:

> There are no other Everglades in the world.
>
> They are, they have always been, one of the unique regions of the earth, remote, never wholly known. Nothing anywhere else is like them: their vast glittering openness, wider than the enormous visible round of the horizon, the racing free saltness and sweetness of their massive winds, under the dazzling blue heights of space. They are unique also in the simplicity, the diversity, the related harmony of the forms of life they enclose. The miracle of the light pours over the green and brown expanse of saw grass and of water, shining and slow-moving below, the grass and water that is the meaning and the central fact of the Everglades of Florida. It is a river of grass.[26]

The ecosystem is held together by fundamental ecological principles that are little understood to this day by the vast majority of Americans. Douglas described this complex web in a way that resonated with her readers, and she elucidated the threats to it in startlingly descriptive detail. She brought her book to its conclusion by describing the massive restoration challenge ahead, appealing to her readers' higher sensibilities, and coaxing them to action:

> The work of the Soil Conservation Service and of the Geological Survey has pointed the way to what should be done. The Army Engineers have now taken the initiative in putting all that research to practical use. How far they will go with

the great plan for the whole Everglades will depend entirely
on the co-operation of the people of the Everglades and their
willingness, at last, to do something intelligent for themselves.
Unless the people act the fires will come again. Overd-
rainage will go on. The soil will shrink and burn and be wasted
and destroyed, in a continuing ruin. The salt will lie in wait.
Yet the springs of fine water had flowed again. The balance still existed between the forces of life and of death.
There is a balance in man also, one which has set against his
greed and his inertia and his foolishness; his courage, his will,
his ability slowly and painfully to learn, and to work together.
Perhaps even in this last hour, in a new relation of useful-
ness and beauty, the vast, magnificent, subtle and unique region
of the Everglades may not be utterly lost.[27]

In sum, Marjory Stoneman Douglas struck a nerve. She made her readers
care. She was able to show how everything affected everything else, how one
perturbation in the ecosystem had untold rippling effects throughout. Her book
was a gift of enlightenment.

For the next 20 years, Douglas tried to build on the success of her Everglades book. In 1952, she published *Road to the Sun*,[28] a novel about land
speculators in South Florida. The book didn't sell particularly well and was
eventually discontinued. Her next project was *Freedom River Florida 1845*,[29] a
thinly veiled depiction of her great-great uncle of Underground Railroad fame.
"What I did, in essence," she said, "was to put old Uncle Levi Coffin out on
the Miami River." Published in 1953, the book sold better. She followed it in
1959 with a similar juvenile book called *Alligator Crossing*.[30] In between these
two works, Marjory was asked by the same company that published her Everglades book to do one on hurricanes. She relished the assignment and in 1958
Hurricane[31] was published. Then, in 1967, she penned *Florida the Long Frontier*,[32] a history of Florida, and in 1973, *Adventures in a Green World—David
Fairchild and Barbour Lathrop*.[33] Although all of these works were more or
less commercially successful, none would come close to having the impact she
made with her treatise on the "river of grass." "There's something about a river
that's a living thing," she mused years later. "It's a stream of history as well as
water."[34]

Friends of the Everglades

The 1960s ushered in a new era of environmentalism throughout the United
States and a new sense of commitment to, and responsibility for, safeguarding
nature. In South Florida, the catalyst for action was an ambitious developer by

the name of Ludwig who proposed building an oil refinery on the shores of lower Biscayne Bay. The idea was so preposterous and met with such widespread opposition that South Florida's environmental ranks swelled with new volunteers.

No sooner had the Ludwig proposal been put to rest than a proposal to build a jetport in the heart of the Everglades was announced. Environmental battles, Douglas was learning quickly, were seldom settled once and for all. At this point in time, however, she remained a writer, not an environmental activist. But that was about to change.

While shopping one day in a local grocery store, Douglas happened upon an outspoken volunteer who worked for Joe Browder, the head of the Miami chapter of the Audubon Society. Browder had been one of the most vocal critics of the oil refinery proposal. As Douglas recounted the conversation years later, she said to the volunteer:

> "'I think you and Joe are doing great work. It's wonderful.'
> She looked me square in the eye and said, 'Yeah, what are
> you doing?' 'Oh me?' I said. 'I wrote the book.' 'That's not
> enough,' she countered. 'We need people to help us.' To get
> out of the conversation, I casually mentioned some platitude
> like 'I'll do whatever I can.'"[35]

Joe Browder quickly followed up and asked Douglas to issue a personal denunciation of the jetport to the press. She demurred by saying that no one would much care what she said about the issue, that such criticism would ring louder if it came from an organization. Undeterred, Crowder challenged Douglas to create that organization, and so she did.

"Friends of the Everglades" became a hard-charging, action-oriented group of concerned citizens. Douglas criss-crossed the state putting her elocution skills to effective use once again to gain support for the fledgling organization. She was joined by several other prominent Miami citizens, and the jetport idea was soon squelched. "Friends of the Everglades" then turned its attention to the general predicament of keeping South Florida wet.

Douglas' oratorical effectiveness was her strongest weapon. As her biographer, John Rothchild, described his first encounter with her at a public meeting in Everglades City:

> Mrs. Douglas was half the size of her fellow speakers and she
> wore huge dark glasses, which along with the huge floppy hat
> made her look like Scarlett O'Hara as played by Igor Stravinsky. When she spoke, everybody stopped slapping [mosquitoes] and more or less came to order. She reminded us all of

our responsibility to nature and I don't remember what else. Her voice had the sobering effect of a one-room schoolmarm's. The tone itself seemed to tame the rowdiest of the local stone crabbers, plus the developers, and the lawyers on both sides. I wonder if it didn't also intimidate the mosquitoes.[36]

Instrumental to this newly charged environmental activism was Art Marshall, a retired World War II military commander who now devoted his life to the study of conservation and water. Marjory secured an obscure copy of Garald Parker's important study of South Florida's hydrologic cycle, and Marshall set about educating the general public about the importance of maintaining a flow of water from the Kissimmee River drainage in Central Florida to the Everglades and Florida Bay in South Florida. Douglas summarized the impact of Marshall's crusade:

> More than any other person, he stretched our idea of the Everglades and how they interact with everything else, which created the most powerful arguments for preserving the water. Self-interest is a more reliable motivation than environmental pity or 'noblesse oblige,' and Marshall accomplished the extraordinary magic of taking the Everglades out of the bleeding-hearts category forever.[37]

By this time in her life, Douglas was well into in her 80s. She was hard-of-hearing and rapidly losing her sight. Yet she would continue her environmental activism for another 20 years. Her biographer described her final years as "flying blind around the world. . .,"[38] with a boundless energy spilling over "onto the unending list of environmental causes that extends from Lake Okeechobee to the Kissimmee River, from the endangered panther to the wood stork, from the coral reefs of Key Largo to the historic houses of Coconut Grove. And she [did] all this as a private citizen."[39]

A Lifetime of Achievement

In 1993, President William Jefferson Clinton awarded Marjory Stoneman Douglas the Presidential Medal of Freedom, the nation's highest civilian honor. She was 103 years old. The citation read in part:

> An extraordinary woman who has devoted her long life to protecting the fragile ecosystem of the Everglades, and to the cause of equal rights for all Americans, Marjory Stoneman Douglas personifies passionate commitment. Her crusade to

preserve and restore the Everglades has enhanced our
Nation's respect for our precious environment, reminding all
of us of nature's delicate balance.[40]

Marjory Stoneman Douglas led a life worth living. In many respects her
personal story mirrored the larger story of the environmental movement in the
United States. In the spring of her career she labored on behalf of social causes,
including the suffrage movement, the plight of undernourished infants,[41] and
Florida legislative reform, the need for which was precipitated by the death of
Martin Tabert. Her work paralleled that of Jane Addams and countless other
social progressives of the time.[42] Later on, in her autumnal years, Douglas took
up the cause of the Equal Rights Amendment, testifying before the Florida legislature in the same way she had testified 50 years earlier on behalf of women's
suffrage. Later still, more than 20 years after she penned her groundbreaking
River of Grass, she metamorphosed into the feisty environmental activist that
characterized the winter of her life.

Douglas' story also parallels what historian Roderick Nash describes as
our liberal democratic tradition,[43] a gradual widening of the circle of ethical
consideration from people to nature to the Earth in its entirety. Douglas
focused much of her early writing on improving the social and economic conditions of disadvantaged South Floridians. Those efforts were followed by her
magnum opus on protecting the Florida Everglades, a book that predated by
two years the publication of Aldo Leopold's *A Sand County Almanac,*[44] and by
fifteen years the publication of Rachel Carson's *Silent Spring.*[45] Finally, in the
twilight of her life, Douglas devoted herself to environmental activism on a
grand scale. Clearly, she served as a faithful midwife to the nascent environmental movement.

The question we are left to ponder is, what was it about Marjory Stoneman
Douglas that allowed her to rise above her inauspicious beginnings, dysfunctional childhood, skeptical and distrustful nature, ill-fated marriage, and bouts
with mental fatigue to accomplish so much of such significance? What was it
that made her special? Part of an answer surely resides in her ability to turn
negative events into positive ones. Most people would have been paralyzed by
the difficulties she encountered in her lifetime, yet Douglas found it within her
to rise above those difficulties in service of a larger cause. Why some people
can do this while others cannot defies easy explanation. Seeing one's own life
as but a fleeting opportunity to contribute to something more enduring, something more ennobling, is a highly admirable quality in a human being.

Marjory Stoneman Douglas had no self-pity. Even though she saw herself
as physically unattractive, she drew on an inner beauty to make her mark on
the world. That ability to make maximum use of her interior gifts allowed her
to persevere in the face of countless exterior obstacles. She had an unflinching

manner about her, an inner confidence that propelled her onward and upward despite the odds. One of Douglas' favorite stories about herself stemmed from a public meeting held on the western edge of Miami when she spoke out against a proposed development project that necessitated draining even more of the Everglades. Like a voice in the wilderness, when she began to speak she was booed by most everyone in the room. "Can't you boo any louder than that?" she egged them on. They booed her again. "That isn't loud enough. Come on, boo me LOUDER."[46] Everyone started laughing. She had broken the tension. The Dade County commission ended up supporting her position and the project was thwarted.

In a 1983 article, Douglas explained her mission:

> It's women's business to be interested in the environment. It's an extended form of housekeeping, isn't it?…I'm just a tough old woman…They can't be rude to me. I have all this white hair. I take advantage of every thing I can—age, hair, disability—because my cause is just. [47]

It was this chutzpah that endeared Marjory Stoneman Douglas to most everyone who met her, including her adversaries. She feared no one, and she welcomed debate. The passion for her cause energized and sustained her, and her tenacity more often than not carried the day. When it came to fighting for the Everglades, she just wouldn't let go. As her biographer summarized her accomplishments, "To have been useful, a useful citizen, has been her greatest pleasure."[48]

The manner in which Douglas went about her day-to-day living was also conducive to the life of the mind. Her possessions were few, her friends many. She was unencumbered by materialism, and she found great joy in the company of books. They took on a life of their own, and she often referred to them as her friends. She called on her books and referenced them in conversation. They were her constant companions. No wonder she relished the writing life. No wonder she found joy in stories. Books lit up her inner life, and her bungalow in Coconut Grove was ideal for silence and the soul searching of a writer. Living alone made it all the easier. She lived a solitary existence but was never lonely.[49]

Marjory Stoneman Douglas died on May 14, 1998 at the age of 108. By the time of her death, she had been honored with most every accolade imaginable by an admiring, appreciative, and loving public. Streets, schools, nature centers, and governmental buildings were named after her. She had earned every bit of it. Douglas was a civil rights activist long before the term was invented. She was a feminist long before that word came into vogue. She was an environmentalist long before environmentalism found its way into our lexicon.

She was a pioneer, and she did all of her pioneering as a private citizen. She took on big business and big government without trepidation. She spoke up at a time in American history when women were not encouraged to do so. She was not just ahead of her time; she was the vanguard of it. Her success fortifies each and every one of us with the knowledge that we, too, can and should take an active role in our participatory democracy. We, too, can and should make a difference through living a life of service.

Douglas did not believe in life after death. Bearing witness to her mother's suffering throughout her childhood made it difficult for her to believe in a caring God. She considered herself an agnostic, but that didn't hamper her enthusiasm for the life she was given one iota. That life was rich enough, full enough, for her. When it ended, eternal rest provided welcome relief.

Given her agnosticism, it is ironic that Marjory Stoneman Douglas lives on today through the imprint she made on the world. She will not soon be forgotten. Her work, the work of an environmentalist, will always be unfinished business. Though the federal government and the State of Florida have recently embarked on an ambitious cooperative effort to restore the health of the Everglades ecosystem, that watery region of South Florida will always remain threatened. Not only is there ongoing environmental damage related to the extensive sugar cane industry and other exhaustive agricultural practices, civic and governmental leaders continue to make every effort to accommodate South Florida's rapidly expanding population. Demographic projections foretell the need to build millions of new homes in the coming years. Guaranteeing those new residents a reliable water source will always be the principal agenda item for South Floridians. For that reason, the life and voice of Marjory Stoneman Douglas is destined to live on, admonishing all who will listen to do what's right by the natural world, and thereby do what's right for humankind.

VI
Democracy Is a Verb

I live on Earth at present, and I don't know what I am.
I know that I am not a category. I am not a thing—a noun.
I seem to be a verb, an evolutionary process—
an integral function of the universe.

—R. Buckminster Fuller[1]

In *The Geography of Thought,* Richard Nisbett, a professor of psychology at the University of Michigan, contrasts Eastern and Western ways of making sense out of the world. In the chapter "Is the World Made Up of Nouns or Verbs?" Nisbett observes that Westerners emphasize nouns that sort phenomena into distinct and separate categories while Asians emphasize verbs that focus on the relationships between those same phenomena.[2]

The lives of Frederick Law Olmsted, Jane Addams, Benton MacKaye, and Marjory Stoneman Douglas illustrate that the noun "democracy," when truly lived, is really a verb. Democracy is civic-mindedness in action. It is people in relationship—not between the one and the many as Western thought would have us believe—but between the part and the whole as Eastern thought teaches us. As R. Buckminster Fuller's poem suggests, democracy, and the people who breathe life into it, are evolving generative processes.

The noted historian, David McCullough, reminds us that the founding fathers intended our democracy to be a government "of the people, by the people, and for the people."[3] Democracy demands that individual citizens take personal responsibility for its proper functioning by getting involved in it. The work is too important to be left to the politicians and their designees. We cannot sit back and allow someone else to do for us what we should be doing for ourselves.

The four historic figures discussed in this book lived the ideal form of a participatory democracy. They were skeptical of experts and politicians. They took matters into their own hands, and they joined hands with others. They also took the time to learn about the issues, to ponder them, and to understand them fully before rendering an opinion. They read widely. They educated themselves.

Thomas Jefferson was right when he said, "Any nation that expects to be ignorant and free expects what never was and never will be."[4] What we gain by living in a participatory democracy is both the opportunity and the obligation to educate ourselves and then to take an active role in our nation's growth and development. Yes, many of us have been prepared for a career, for a specialization, and it is important that we do that specialized work well. But that is only part of the story. The purpose of an education is not only to prepare us for a job. It is to prepare us to be enlightened, socially responsible, engaged citizens.

In this concluding chapter, we direct your attention to the larger, unfolding story of our nation and the role you can and should play in it. This requires fully understanding yourself as an interdependent part of the whole and seeing your life as an opportunity to contribute to something much larger and more enduring than yourself. It also requires you to appreciate that a life worth living is largely a function of service to others.

Life as Synecdoche

In *From These Beginnings: a Biographical Approach to American History,* Roderick Nash and Gregory Graves tell America's story through the lives of a handful of its most interesting people, including Christopher Columbus, Benjamin Franklin, Abigail Adams, and Thomas Jefferson.[5] Underlying this biographical approach to American history is the belief that recounting the stories of people who affected and were affected by their times is an engaging way to learn about the past in preparation for the future. The approach assumes that an individual story can serve as a synecdoche, a representation of a larger story. This approach has been ours as well.

Considered collectively, the lives of Frederick Law Olmsted, Jane Addams, Benton MacKaye, and Marjory Stoneman Douglas spanned most of the history of the United States of America—from 1822 until 1998. The times in which they lived were influenced greatly by westward expansion, a growing sense of nationalism, the rise of urbanization, the development of an industrialized economy, a concern for social reform, and the emergence of environmentalism. Their personal contributions to the nation's larger emerging story include Olmsted's efforts to give urbanites a natural respite from the inhuman strictures of city living, Addams' efforts to make city life more bearable for the underprivileged, MacKaye's efforts to save part of the natural world for future generations, and Douglas' efforts to communicate the importance of maintaining an ecosystem's integrity to sustain all life. Each of these people lived the nation's story through their own service living.

The philosopher Oliver Reiser reasons that not one of us is without the power to contribute to the making of the future, and that not one of us is free from the responsibility for doing so.[6] No matter what we do with our lives, we influence the future. We can choose to sit on the sidelines and leave the nation's work to others, or we can think deeply about what matters and then roll up our sleeves and do something about it. Either way—through acts of omission or commission—we are contributing to the future. That responsibility cannot be escaped.

Our Expanding Liberal Democratic Tradition

What, then, matters? For us, it is leaving the world a better place for all our children and our children's children. This demands taking the future seriously. It also demands taking the long view and thinking through the consequences of our actions before we act. It demands paying less attention to quarterly reports that are measured in three month increments and more attention to generational outcomes that are measured in lifetimes. It demands resisting self-indulgence and exercising restraint out of a concern for others. It demands expressing conscious appreciation of the fact that we are part of a larger community of life that will exist long after we are gone, and it demands living up to the obligation to conduct ourselves in a manner befitting that appreciation. Ultimately, what it demands from us is ethical conduct characterized by service living.

In *A Sand County Almanac,* Aldo Leopold contends that our progress as a species can be measured by the degree to which we extend ethical consideration outward from the self and others to the land and all of its creatures.[7] The lives of Frederick Law Olmsted, Jane Addams, Benton MacKaye, and Marjory Stoneman Douglas were steeped in that tradition of expanding ethical consideration. Quite independent of one another, they shared a common familial history of being against slavery and in favor of social reform. As they matured they extended their ethical thinking outward. Examined together, their lives mirrored the country's gradual awakening to the possibility of seeing humankind, as Leopold wanted us to see ourselves, as plain members and citizens of the land community. In the cases of Olmsted and Addams, they extended ethical consideration to less fortunate people. In the cases of MacKaye and Douglas, they extended ethical consideration to nature and communities.

The invitation to join in this expanding liberal democratic tradition is open to each of us. Our challenge is to "step up to the plate" and take our turn at doing something for the public good. While we can offer no specific formula for success, we can once again direct attention to the experiences of our four historic personages. Despite their individual differences, they shared several common characteristics that allowed them to rise above their own circumstances to live a life of public service.

Reaching Skyward

One of the most interesting aspects of the lives of these four people is how their youthful experiences shaped and molded their respective life paths. None of them had it easy. Frederick Law Olmsted lost his mother when he was three. Jane Addams lost her mother when she was two. Benton MacKaye lost his father when he was 15, and Marjory Stoneman Douglas' father left the household when she was five. As young people, each one of them had to deal with major losses, and each one of them had to adjust and adapt as best they could.

Among other things, they took refuge in books. Rather than closing themselves off from the world as a way of coping with their grief, they opened themselves up to it through reading. They expanded their horizons and began to explore life's possibilities. This was especially evident in the lives of Jane Addams and Marjory Stoneman Douglas. Reading stimulated their imaginations and expanded their world views. This was particularly important for them at a time in American history when girls were discouraged from "rocking the boat" and thinking for themselves.

Travel also played an important role in each of their lives. From Olmsted's seafaring, to Addams' European journeys, to MacKaye's personal "expeditions," to Douglas' Wellesley College days, they each turned outward to learn more about the world. Exposure to other lands, other cultures, and other ways of knowing equipped them with a perspective that lent itself to lifelong learning, exploration, and risk-taking. They learned to take life on rather than recoiling from it.

Their introductions to the plight of the economically, socially, and culturally disadvantaged when they were young were especially important. What could have been a life of learning in the abstract was replaced by seeing and experiencing life's problems up close and personal. Having done so, it was impossible later on in life for these four citizens to ignore what was going on around them. Experiential learning during their formative years taught them to be civic-minded, action-oriented adults.

They had the courage to set their thoughts before the public, ready to absorb inevitable criticism. They applied their learning to shaping the world, and they shared their ideas about the issues they addressed and the actions they undertook, thereby broadening their impact and leaving a written legacy from which succeeding generations could benefit.

The principal message this collection of experiences holds for us is to meet life "head on," to embrace self-doubts, insecurities, and anxieties, and give life a go. What, after all, is the alternative? Not getting involved and sitting on the sidelines while life passes us by can hardly be called living. Olmsted, Addams, MacKaye, and Douglas understood this, whether they articulated it or not. They consciously chose a life of action, engagement, and service living. Anything less would have disappointed them.

Also apparent from reading their stories was that life, in many respects, was a struggle for them. They developed character by overcoming adversity and taking the long view of things. All of them took years to find their life's calling, and the marks they made on the world were the result of a lifetime of service. Amidst the ups and downs of their everyday lives they demonstrated strength and perseverance. This is not easy to do in a day and age when we are acculturated into expecting instant gratification. To devote our lives to causes that may yield little, if any, tangible personal rewards in this lifetime runs counter to mainstream "me-first" thinking. It borders on missionary zeal, and it requires a faith that views public service as worthy.

But, of course, this is the heart of what we have been saying throughout this book. It is our private selves in service of the public good that defines a life worth living. To be a public servant is a noble undertaking. Whether we are government employees or private citizens, we share the same work. We are nation builders. Whether we work alone or in groups, our mission is the same— *lifelong action that contributes to the health and well-being of all living things.* In this regard, the part of each of us that lives on through our lasting words and deeds is what matters. Conducting ourselves in the light of this reality is the litmus test of our existence. It is no mean feat given our human frailties and proclivities. As the poet Robert Browning reminds us, "Ah, but a man's reach should exceed his grasp, or what's a heaven for?"

The Ripple Effect

In *Good Work,*[8] Howard Gardner, Mihaly Csikszentmihalyi, and William Damon examine the ethics of the work world. Contrary to what we might expect, what they find leaves them optimistic about the possibility of combining the independence of thought and action that energizes individual human creativity and productivity with the interdependence that defines community life. Good work—work of expert quality that benefits the broader society—is a reasonable goal for each of us.[9] The challenge is to raise people who are ready and willing to do good work. Ryan Hreljac of Kemptville, Ontario, Canada is a great example.

> When he was six years old, Ryan learned from his teacher that children in Africa often must walk miles each day to find water. Some even die from drinking bad water, his teacher said. So Ryan decided to act. He did chores for his parents, Susan and Mark, and for neighbors. He spoke to schools, churches, and clubs about his goal. The word spread, and donations began coming in. After several months of hard work, Ryan had raised $2,000, enough to dig one well…After the first well, "the ripple effect took over," Ryan says, "and one goal led to another." With adult help, he founded Ryan's Well Foundation…to educate people about the vital importance of water. Now the foundation has raised more than $1.5 million and built 255 wells that serve more than 427,000 people in 12 countries…Asked if he ever feels discouraged that

many people still lack good water, Ryan says, "It's important to be an optimist. When people are dying on the other side of the world, to sit in your house and say, 'I can't really help,' that's not the person I want to be."[10]

Good Work's authors emphasize the development of individual competence and character while simultaneously encouraging differentiation (autonomous individuality) and integration (meaningful connectedness to others) in young people. They point out that differentiation is traditionally the highest goal of human development in Western cultures while integration is traditionally the highest goal of human development in Eastern cultures. They call for a harmonious blending of the two to reach our human potential.[11] Rightly understood, differentiation and integration merge individualism and communalism in a way that serves the common good. Therein lies the essence of service living.

Looking out across this vast country of ours, watching the evening news, or reading the daily newspaper, it is easy to conclude that the business of America is surely business. America, however, is much more than a marketplace. It is a grand experiment in democratic living that requires coupling self-interest with the public interest in a way that serves both the individual and the community in the long run. To succeed, democracy depends on citizens like Ryan Hreljac.

There are strong parallels between "good work" and "service living." They both hinge on ethical consideration, they both depend on acknowledging our connectedness to a cause larger than ourselves, and they both stress the importance of effort expended over time. This parallel thinking is a good sign. It suggests we may be getting somewhere with our expanding liberal democratic tradition. Broadening our intellectual, emotional, and spiritual horizons reveals the possibilities for a more connected and caring world after all, a world grounded in ecological reality.

Now is the time to do our own good work. Having read about Frederick Law Olmsted, Jane Addams, Benton MacKaye, and Marjory Stoneman Douglas, we can appreciate that these were imperfect human beings who found the strength within themselves to go beyond their imperfections to make remarkable and lasting impacts on the world. While their lives were transitory, their achievements were not. As we consider the mark we would like to leave upon the world, we should not disappoint our founding fathers and mothers. Neither should we disappoint Frederick Law Olmsted, Jane Addams, Benton MacKaye, and Marjory Stoneman Douglas. But most important of all, we should not disappoint the part of each of us that is connected to the everlasting community of life. For the sake of our democracy and our future, we must be the best possible citizens we can be. In so doing we will create a meaningful and fulfilling existence for ourselves. The path is paved with service living.

VII
Afterword:
Why We Chose Frederick Law Olmsted, Jane Addams, Benton MacKaye, and Marjory Stoneman Douglas

We began this project with our personal attractions to historic figures who we believed had made significant contributions to advancing the public good. We each had our own reasons for selecting our special people, and as you are about to see, those reasons were highly personal. Our challenge was to weave their stories together in a way that reflected our individual interests while simultaneously communicating the common lessons their stories taught.

Frederick Law Olmsted: Doug Wellman

Although I had visited Central Park and Niagara Falls, I didn't truly discover Frederick Law Olmsted until, as a new assistant professor, I was assigned responsibility for teaching a large introductory undergraduate course in outdoor recreation. My understanding of both content and pedagogy was limited, and the first several years were challenging. Through lots of reading, I built my knowledge of the history of American park and recreation policy. My growing command of content enabled me to move from lecturing to more interactive forms of teaching. To allow more class time for case studies, debates, and other active learning exercises, I transcribed my lecture notes and assigned them as homework. My goal in the course was for students to leave with an understanding of the policy process and an appreciation for its human dimensions, since some of them might be involved in recreation policy development or implementation as professionals or citizens. To make the big ideas real and memorable, my notes relied heavily on biography and narrative. Those notes led to a book contract and a life-changing five-year learning experience that resulted in the publication of *Wildland Recreation Policy: An Introduction* in 1987.[1]

As the book took shape, Olmsted assumed an increasingly important position. Joseph Sax's stimulating *Mountains without Handrails: Reflections on the National Parks*[2] provided me with my first deep drink of Olmsted's thinking and its significance for the ongoing struggle between preservation and development in our national parks. Sax's book led me to Laura Wood Roper's wonderful biography, *FLO: a Biography of Frederick Law Olmsted*.[3] Roper set

Olmsted's ideas about national parks in the context of his life and helped me understand the experiences that led to his philosophy on public park planning and management. I came away from Roper's biography full of respect for Olmsted's democratic idealism and his persistence in overcoming adversity.

Seventeen years after *Wildland Recreation Policy* was published, Dennis Propst and I brought out a second edition. As part of my work on the second edition, I read new literature on key historical figures, including Olmsted. One of my great discoveries was Witold Rybczynski's insightful and provocative biography, *A Clearing in the Distance: Frederick Law Olmsted and America in the 19th Century.*[4] Reading Rybczynski's book deepened my understanding of Olmsted's democratic idealism. It also complemented my longstanding interest in how resource management agencies interact with the public. I had taken my first pass at this topic in my master's thesis, but most of my work came in the late 1980s when I joined with Terry Tipple of Virginia Tech's Center for Public Administration and Policy in a series of studies of how resource management professionals work with citizens in our democracy.[5]

I was drawn to Olmsted not from direct experience with his work, but from a growing appreciation for the liberality and depth of his thinking, his lifelong concern for social justice, his indomitable character, his integrity, and his willingness to take risks. Realizing that this heroic figure was also very human—suffering bouts of depression, fretting about how others perceived him and his profession, practicing manipulation on occasion—only deepened my admiration of his good qualities.

Jane Addams: Karla Henderson

I'm not sure when I first heard Jane Addams' name. It was likely when I was in graduate school taking a class on nonprofit organizations. We visited two sites in Minneapolis that had been settlement houses. You couldn't talk about settlement houses without reference to Chicago's Hull House. It was not the first settlement house, but it was certainly the most famous because of Addams.

My fascination with Addams began with two serendipitous occurrences at the University of Wisconsin-Madison (UW-M), my inaugural faculty post. First, UW-M had a series of rooms in the student center named after Addams and her colleagues from Hull House. I was reminded of her often when I walked by "her" room. Second, during this same time I became a "born again" feminist. I always thought I was a feminist but had never asked some of the most obvious critical questions about the park and recreation profession that should have been asked from a feminist perspective. Other than Addams, for example, who were our female leaders? Although I knew Addams must have been an important person, I really had no idea what she had actually done in terms of her contribution to my field. I also wondered what she had done to warrant the notoriety that other women in my field lacked.

I was not the only one raising these questions. Susan Hudson wrote an essay in 1982 asking, "Who was our mother?"[1] I didn't know the answer. For me, the place to start was with the life of Addams, which I began to explore in 1982. I read many of her books and soon published an article in the *Journal of Physical Education, Recreation, and Dance*[2] that gave me the chance to "think out loud" and share what I had learned with others. Addams became my personal heroine. If I could "have dinner with someone living or dead and spend an evening together talking," Addams would be that person. Over the years, I have explored the lives of several other women who were integral to our profession,[3] but none have had Addams' charisma.

I enjoy reading history. I have found some feminist history particularly compelling because it is not focused on chronology per se but on the values that influenced people's everyday lives. Often women are described in history by what they contributed to traditional (i.e., male) values. A transitional history of women and their lives views their cultural contributions during particular historical times. Thus, while birth, education, significant achievements, and death are important milestones in a famous individual's life, I chose to write about Addams because of the cultural roles she played throughout her life. Describing her as a community organizer, reformer, social theorist, author, urban planner, feminist, and pacifist were most interesting to me. I aspire to be like Addams because of her ability to excel in these roles. I relate to those characteristics more so than to the specific history and times that framed Addams' life.

Having examined the life of Addams when I was younger, fresher, and perhaps more idealistic was inspiring to me. Coming back to visit her life again in the context of the wisdom and experience I have gained in the past 25 years makes me no less awed by her abilities to motivate others, write, and stand up for her beliefs. I continue to find Addams' story relevant to today's world in light of peace and war issues and urban concerns. I am more inspired by her persona now than ever before. I still wish I could have dinner with her and listen to what she would have to say about the state of our country and world today.

Benton MacKaye: Roger Moore

Two factors led to my decision to better understand and write about the life and accomplishments of Benton MacKaye. One was personal and the other professional.

The Boy Scout troop I belonged to many years ago was all about hiking and camping. We took local day hikes, weekend treks, and extended summer "expeditions" in New Hampshire, Pennsylvania, and West Virginia, most of them on the Appalachian Trail. We quickly concluded that the Appalachian

Trail was the greatest of all trails. I remember standing near its midpoint during one of those trips and looking north and then south as I thought about the startling fact that someone could actually hike a thousand miles in either direction following those simple, white paint blazes. Like so many other hikers, I began to dream of someday "thru-hiking" the entire Appalachian Trail, a dream that came true for me in 1973.

Somewhere on one of those early Boy Scout "expeditions," I learned that MacKaye was the one who conceived of this 2,175-mile wilderness footpath. Many years passed before I understood how this amazing idea moved from his head to reality, but I never forgot that MacKaye was somehow the "father" of the Appalachian Trail, a place and an idea that were very important to me.

The other factor in my decision to write about MacKaye was more professional, although intertwined with enjoying and appreciating "his" trail. My Appalachian Trail thru-hike led directly to a seasonal job working on trails in New Hampshire, which led to a full-time position working primarily on the National Park Service Appalachian Trail protection program. Those experiences led to graduate school and ultimately to my career as a professor in parks and recreation in which I frequently conduct research on trails and trail users.

My career has now come full circle, leading me to two terms on the Board of Directors of the Appalachian Trail Conservancy, the nonprofit organization MacKaye helped found in 1925. My decision to serve was partly motivated by a desire to give something back to the Appalachian Trail and its stewards who had given so much to me. Many "trails" intersect and sometimes parallel the Appalachian Trail, and my career path has been one of them.

Another factor connecting me to MacKaye has to do with one of the tools he used to make his lasting impact—writing. We professors generally write for academic journals, and they are certainly important outlets for going public with our thinking. But our carefully crafted words often seem to disappear into thin air. MacKaye, on the other hand, published a journal article that managed to do something very unusual—it led to the creation of the most famous trail on earth. His writing helped spark concerted action by tens of thousands of volunteers to look after the trail, and through their efforts, to ensure the enjoyment of generations of hikers and nature lovers. The most common sentence describing the origins of the Appalachian Trail usually reads something like this, "...the idea for the Appalachian Trail was proposed by Benton MacKaye in 1921 in *The Journal of the American Institute of Architects*."[1]

I have always been encouraged that MacKaye's prolific writings (and actions) on trails, wilderness, open space protection, regional planning, community involvement, and a host of other topics important to me have been, and continue to be, effective and beneficial. His example helps remind me that each of us can make the world "more habitable," as he would have said, even under what might seem unlikely circumstances and means. I, too, would like to make such a difference. Honoring the legacy of Benton MacKaye is one way of doing so.

Marjory Stoneman Douglas: Dan Dustin

Writing about Marjory Stoneman Douglas has been a way for me to put an exclamation point on my nine-year "visit" to South Florida. I moved there from California in 1997 to look after my 90-year-old mother when my father died. I lived in Port Charlotte on the Gulf Coast to be near my mother, and I taught at Florida International University in Miami on the Atlantic Coast to pay the bills. On my weekly treks to and fro, the geographer in me grew fascinated with what lies between Port Charlotte and Miami—the Everglades, a vast preserve chock full of alligators, snakes, and water birds. I learned to appreciate the "river of grass," and I wanted to better understand its ecology. Through her writing, Douglas became one of my principal teachers, along with black-and-white landscape photographer Clyde Butcher and his wife Niki, and Buffalo Tiger and Ernie Redwing of the Miccosukee Tribe. Honoring my teachers explains part of my motivation for wanting to be a part of this book. The chance to work with Doug Wellman, Karla Henderson, and Roger Moore explains a bit more. My love for writing explains the rest.

I have always been intrigued by the proposition that the pen is mightier than the sword. Ever since I was a high school journalism student, I have been trying to live up to the promise of that proposition. It has not been easy. One of the first bits of advice I received about putting pen to paper was "Writing is the process of turning blood into ink."[1] And that has been my experience. Writing—for me at least—is a slow, painstaking process.

While I have published extensively, I have seldom considered what I've written to be real writing. My reverence for words, and for people who weave them together in the most creative and compelling fashion, is too great to think I could ever become one of them. Surely there must be something perfect about these people that accounts for their perfect writing. I have made it my business to study selected writers from time to time to identify the source of their perfection.

I have yet to find that wellspring. On the contrary, what I've found has surprised me. I've found flawed and occasionally troubled individuals who have simply made it their habit to turn "blood into ink." They include Edward Abbey, Wallace Stegner, Farley Mowat, and now Marjory Stoneman Douglas. While I confess to some disappointment in finding out that my perfect writers are not perfect people, I have also derived considerable hope from examining their lives that real writing is not beyond me.

What we see when we read other people's published work is but the final draft. We don't see the blood, the sweat, or the tears that preceded it. We don't see the fits and starts, the writing blocks, or the editorial revisions that were all part of the struggle to get something right on paper. We don't see the magnitude of the effort. What we read is so polished that we can't imagine it ever being otherwise. We assume that it must have come easily, and, therefore, that what real writers do is beyond us. I don't know why we do this to ourselves. Perhaps it gives us the excuse not to engage in the struggle of writing in the first place.

When you read about the life of Marjory Stoneman Douglas, you see how mistaken our assumptions can be. Nothing was easy about the life or the writing of this firefly of a woman, darting here and there, in her wide-brimmed floppy hat and oversized sunglasses. She had her demons. She had her self-doubts. She had her setbacks. Yet she persevered. Furthermore, late in life, when she could have called it quits, when she could have rested on her laurels, when her hearing and eyesight were failing, she found the strength of character to employ her pen and voice even more ardently as an environmental activist. That Marjory Stoneman Douglas made a difference to the very end only goes to show that we imperfect human beings can have our moments of perfection too, if only we would try.

VIII
Notes

I: Why Service Living?

1. Olson, S. (1977). *Reflections from the north country.* New York, NY: Alfred A. Knopf, p. 59.
2. Dustin, D., McAvoy, L., and Schultz, J. (2002). *Stewards of access/ custodians of choice: A philosophical foundation for the park and recreation profession.* Champaign, IL: Sagamore Publishing, Inc.
3. Personal communication from Patti Clayton at North Carolina State University, December 2, 2007.
4. Putnam, R. (2000). *Bowling alone: The collapse and revival of American community.* New York: Simon and Schuster.
5. Bellah, R., Madsen, R., Sullivan, W., Swindler, A., and Tipton, S. (1985). *Habits of the heart: Individualism and commitment in American life.* Berkeley, CA: University of California Press.
6. de Tocqueville, A. (1969). *Democracy in America.* (Translated by G. Lawrence, edited by J. Mayer). New York: Doubleday, Anchor Books.
7. Bellah et al., p. xiii
8. ibid.
9. Bellah, R., Madsen, R., Sullivan, W., Swindler, A., and Tipton, S. (1996). *Habits of the heart: Individualism and commitment in American life,* 2nd Edition. Berkeley, CA: University of California Press, pp. vii–viii.
10. Smith, A. (1937). An inquiry into the nature and causes of the wealth of nations. New York: The Modern Library.
11. Bellah, et al. (1996), p. xiii.
12. Thurow, L. (1995). Companies merge; families break up. *New York Times,* September 3.
13. Bellah, et al. (1996), p. xiii.
14. Goodman, E. (2007). The CEO was big in shelter. *Raleigh News and Observer,* January 16.
15. Bellah, et al. (1996), p. xv.
16. Veblen, T. (1934). *The theory of the leisure class: An economic study of institutions.* New York: Modern Library.
17. Bellah, et al. (1996), p. 253.
18. ibid., p. 257.
19. Tritch, T. (2006). The rise of the super-rich. *New York Times,* July 19.
20. Roszak, T., Gomes, M., and Kanner, A. (Eds.). (1995). *Ecopsychology: Restoring the earth/healing the mind.* San Francisco, CA: Sierra Club Books.

21. Yankelovich, D. (1981). *New rules: Searching for self-fulfillment in a world turned upside down*. New York: Random House.
22. Elgin, D. (1993). *Voluntary simplicity*. New York: William Morrow
23. ibid., p. 59.
24. Bellah, et al. (1996), p. 270.

II: Painting with Lakes and Wooded Slopes: The Democratic Artistry of Frederick Law Olmsted

1. Rybczynski, W. (1999). *A clearing in the distance: Frederick Law Olmsted and America in the nineteenth century*. New York: Scribner, p. 394. Witold Rybczynski's masterful and eminently readable biography is the primary source for this chapter. Only quotations are footnoted.
2. Douthat, R. (2006). They Made America. *The Atlantic, 298*(5):59–78.
3. Rybczynski, p. 23.
4. ibid. p. 31.
5. ibid. p. 32
6 Olmsted, F. L. (1859). *Walks and talks of an American farmer in England*. Columbus, OH: Jos. H. Riley and Company, p. v.
7. ibid. p. 87.
8. Roper, L. (1973). *FLO: A biography of Frederick Law Olmsted*. Baltimore: Johns Hopkins University Press, p. 70.
9. ibid., p. 68–69.
10. ibid., p. 71.
11. ibid., p. 93.
12. Rybczynski, p. 113.
13. ibid. p. 119.
14. ibid. p. 121.
15. ibid., p. 139.
16. Rosenzweig, R. and Blackmar, E. (1992). *The park and the people: A history of Central Park*. Ithaca, NY: Cornell University Press, pp. 15–58.
17. Roper, pp. 130.
18. Rybczynski, p. 174. Rosenzweig and Blackmar note that critics of the grid plan for Manhattan had been complaining about its monotony for some time before Olmsted and Vaux's plan. Whatever credit Olmsted should be given for the idea of breaking that monotony with the park, he and Vaux were at least attuned to the concerns and able to articulate the park's benefits in addressing them.
19. ibid. p. 165.
20. ibid.

21. ibid. p. 210.
22. ibid. p. 217.
23. ibid., p. 213.
24. ibid. p. 236
25. ibid. p. 237.
26. The large, unified Yosemite National Park we now know did not come to be for another 42 years and required two policy actions: first, in 1890, Congress passed the Yosemite National Park forest reservation, thereby surrounding the small 1864 grant with a huge natural area; and second, in 1906, California returned the small grant of valley and grove to the federal government.
27. Rybczynski p. 254.
28. ibid.
29. Roper, p. 253.
30. ibid. p. xiv.
31. ibid., p. 268.
32. Olmsted, F. (1865). Yosemite and the Mariposa Grove: A Preliminary Report. (http://www.yosemite.ca.us/library/olmsted/report.html)
33. ibid.
34. Sax, J. (1980). *Mountains without handrails: Reflections on the national parks.* Ann Arbor: The University of Michigan Press, p. 20.
35. ibid.
36. ibid., p. 21.
37. Olmsted.
38. Roper, p. 285.
39. Sax, pp. 24–25.
40. http://en.wikipedia.org/wiki/frederick_law_olmsted.
41. Rybczynski, p. 397.
42. Lawson, E. (2003). *The devil in the white city: Murder, magic, and madness at the fair that changed America.* New York: Vintage Books, 228 (workforce), 254 (electricity use).
43. Roper, p. xiv.

III: Employing Sympathetic Knowledge: Jane Addams of Chicago's Hull House

1. Internet Encyclopedia of Philosophy. (n.d.) Jane Addams (1860–1935). Retrieved on December 20, 2006 from http://www.iep.utm.edu/a/addamsj.htm
2. Fradin, J. and Fradin, D. (2006). *Jane Addams: Champion of democracy.* New York, NY: Clarion Books.

3. Davis, A. and McCree, M. (1969). *Eighty years at Hull House.* Chicago, IL: Quadrangle Books.
4. Fradin and Fradin (2006).
5. Henderson, K., Bialeschki, D., Shaw, S., and Freysinger, V. (1996). *Both gains and gaps: Feminist perspectives on women's leisure.* State College, PA: Venture Publishing, Inc.
6. Bettis, N. (n.d.). Jane Addams 1860–1935. Retrieved on December 20, 2006 from http://www.webster.edu/~woolflm/janeaddams.html
7. Kent, D. (1992). *The story of Jane Addams—Hull House.* Chicago, IL: Children's Press.
8. ibid. p. 5.
9. Fradin and Fradin (2006).
10. Knight, L. (2005). *Citizen: Jane Addams and the struggle for democracy.* Chicago, IL: The University of Chicago Press.
11. Chronology of Jane Addams' Life. Retrieved on December 20, 2006 from http://www.uic.edu/jaddams/hull/ja_chronology.html
12. Fradin and Fradin (2006).
13. Chronology of Jane Addams' Life (n.d.).
14. Fradin and Fradin (2006), p. 2.
15. ibid.
16. ibid.
17. Knight, L. (2005).
18. Fradin and Fradin (2006).
19. Kent, D. (1992).
20. Chronology of Jane Addams' Life (n.d.).
21. Bettis, N. (n.d.).
22. Kent, D. (1992).
23. Fradin and Fradin (2006).
24. Addams, J. (1910). *Twenty years at Hull House.* New York, NY: The Macmillan Company.
25. Knight, L. (2005).
26. Fradin and Fradin (2006).
27. America's Library. (n.d.) Jane Addams, the peacemaker. Retrieved on December 20, 2006 from http://www.americaslibrary.gov/cgi-bin/page.cgi/aa/activists/addams/peace_3
28. Fradin and Fradin (2006), p. 178.
29. ibid.
30. ibid.
31. Kent, D. (1992).
32. National Archives. (n.d.) Jane Addams. Retrieved on December 20, 2006 from http://www.spartacus.schoolnet.co.uk?USAaddams.htm
33. Fradin and Fradin (2006), pp. 190–191.

34. About Women's History. (n.d.) Jane Addams quotes. Retrieved on December 20, 2006 from http:/womenshistory.about.com/od/quotes/a/jane_addams.htm
35. ibid.
36. ibid.
37. Chronology of Jane Addams' Life (n.d.).
38. Fradin and Fradin (2006).
39. Tims, M. (1961). *Jane Addams of Hull House 1860–1935*. London: George Allen and Unwin Ltd. p. 13.
40. National Archives (n.d.).
41. Addams, J. (1972; reprint of 1909 edition). *The spirit of youth and city streets*. Urbana, IL: University of Illinois Press.
42. Stubblefield, H. and Hunt, T. (n.d.) The case of Jane Addams and the revisionist historians: A framework for writing a history of adult education. Unpublished paper.
43. Knight, L. (2005).
44. ibid. p. 242.
45. Stubblefield and Hunt (n.d.).
46. Chronology of Jane Addams' Life.
47. Fradin and Fradin (2006).
48. Women in History (n.d.) Jane Addams. Retrieved on December 20, 2006 from http://www.lkwdpl.org/wihohio/adda-jan.htm
49. Brown, V. (2001). Jane Addams in Women Building Chicago 1790–1990: A biographical dictionary. Retrieved on December 20, 2006 from http://tigger.uic.edu/htbin/cgiwrap/bin/urbnexp/main.cgi?file=new/show_doc_search.ptt
50. Henderson, K. (1982). Jane Addams: Pioneer in leisure services. *Journal of Physical Education, Recreation, and Dance, 53*(2): 42–46.
51. Farrell, J. (1967). *Beloved lady: a history of Jane Addams' ideas on reform and peace*. Baltimore, MD: The John Hopkins Press.
52. Addams, J. (1972; reprint of 1909 edition).
53. ibid. p. 4.
54. Henderson, K. (1982).
55. Addams, J. (1972; reprint of 1909 edition), p. 103.
56. Farrell, J. (1967), p. 365.
57. ibid.
58. Henderson, K. (1982).
59. Farrell, J. (1967).
60. Addams, J. (1960). *The centennial reader*. New York, NY: The Macmillan Company, p. 435.
61. Henderson, et al. (1996).
62. Knight, L. (2005).

63. Henderson, K. (1982).
64. Women in History (n.d.).
65. Chronology of Jane Addams' Life (n.d.).
66. ibid.
67. Women in History (n.d.).
68. National Archives (n.d.).
69. ibid.
70. Internet Encyclopedia of Philosophy (n.d.). Retrieved on December 20, 2006 from http://www.iep.utm.edu/a/addamsj.htm

IV: A Wilderness Pathfinder: Benton MacKaye and the Appalachian Trail

1. This section draws heavily on a marvelous biography of MacKaye: Anderson, L. (2002). *Benton MacKaye: Conservationist, planner, and creator of the Appalachian Trail*. Baltimore, MD: Johns Hopkins Press.
2. Lippmann, W. (1911). As quoted in Anderson, L. (2002), pp. 21–22.
3. Anderson, L. (2002), p. 36.
4. MacKaye, B. (1919). *Employment and natural resources*. U.S. Department of Labor, Office of the Secretary.
5. MacKaye, B. (1921). An Appalachian Trail: A Project in Regional Planning. *Journal of the American Institute of Architects*. (October): 325–330.
6. MacKaye, B. (1991). *The new exploration: A philosophy of regional planning*. Urbana, IL: University of Illinois and Appalachian Trail Conference.
7. Anderson, L. (2002), p. 273.
8. MacKaye, B. (n.d.). *Geotechnics of North America*. Unpublished manuscript. (Copy on file at the Dartmouth College Library.)
9. MacKaye, B. (1968). *From geography to geotechnics*. Urbana-Champaign, IL: University of Illinois Press (edited by Paul T. Bryant).
10. MacKaye, B. (1969). *Expedition nine: A return to a region*. The Wilderness Society.
11. Anderson, L. (2002), p. 76.
12. Mumford, L. (1927). As quoted in Anderson, L. (2002), p. 4.
13. Stein, C. As quoted in Anderson, L. (2002), p. 150.
14. Anderson, L. (2002), p. 146.
15. King, B. (2000, July). Trail Years: A History of ATC. *Appalachian Trailway News*, Special 75th Anniversary Issue, p. 8.
16. ibid. p. 11.
17. Mumford, L. (1976). Benton MacKaye as Regional Planner. *Living Wilderness*, *39*(132): 17.

18. MacKaye, B. (September, 1935). Why the Appalachian Trail. *Living Wilderness, 1:* 7–8. As quoted in Anderson, L. (2002), p. 280.
19. MacKaye, B. (1935). Personal correspondence as quoted in Anderson, L. (2002), p. 281.
20. MacKaye, B. (1934). (Draft Copy) Invitation to Help Organize a Group to Preserve the American Wilderness. As quoted in Anderson, L. (2002), p. 274.
21. Mumford, L. (1976), p. 17.
22. Bryant, P. (1976). MacKaye as Writer. *Living Wilderness, 39*(132): 33.
23. Mumford, L. (1976), p. 15.
24. MacKaye, B. (1968), pp. 22–24.
25. Gutheim, F. (1976). Saying It and Doing It. *Living Wilderness, 39*(132): 31.
26. Bryant, P. (1976), pp. 31–33.
27. Bryant, P. (1968). In Introduction to, MacKaye, B. (1968). *From geography to geotechnics.* Urbana-Champaign, IL: University of Illinois Press, pp. 1–8.
28. MacKaye, B. (1968), p. 46.
29. Chase, S. (1976). My Friend Benton. *Living Wilderness, 39*(132): 17.
30. MacKaye, B. (1968), p. 174.
31. ibid. pp. 169–179.
32. ibid. p. 179.
33. Gutheim, F. (1976), p. 31.
34. Bryant, P. (1976), p. 31.
35. ibid. p. 33.
36. MacKaye, B. (1968), p. 88.
37. Bryant, P. (1976), p. 32.
38. Howes, R. (1976). The Knoxville Years. *Living Wilderness, 39*(132): 24.
39. Durham, C. (1976). A View from the Earldom. *Living Wilderness, 39*(132): 26.
40. Howes, R. (1976), p. 23.
41. Mumford, L. (1976), p. 13.
42. Oehser, P. (1976). A Yankee Trailblazer. *Living Wilderness, 39*(132): 8.
43. Anderson, L. (2002), p. 369.
44. Mumford, L. (1932). Personal correspondence as quoted in Anderson, L. (2002), p. 228.
45. Anderson, L. (2002), ibid. p. 51.
46. Mumford, L. (1976), p. 14.
47. MacKaye, B. (1968), p. 162.
48. ibid.
49. Anderson, L. (2002), pp. 368-369.

V: Our Lady of the Glades: Marjory Stoneman Douglas and Florida's "River of Grass"

1. McKibben, W. (2006). In B. Lopez (Ed.), *Home ground: Language for an American landscape*. San Antonio, TX: Trinity University Press, p. 128.
2. Douglas, M. (1947). *The Everglades: River of grass*. Port Salerno, FL: Florida Classics Library.
3. Douglas, M. (with J. Rothchild) (1987). *Marjory Stoneman Douglas: Voice of the river*. Sarasota, FL: Pineapple Press, Inc. pp. 43–44.
4. ibid. p. 57.
5. ibid. p. 68.
6. ibid. p. 81.
7. ibid. p. 78.
8. ibid. p. 83.
9. ibid. p. 84.
10. ibid. p. 85.
11. ibid. p. 86.
12. ibid. p. 89.
13. ibid. p. 85.
14. ibid. p. 96.
15. ibid. p. 107.
16. ibid. p. 127.
17. Douglas, M. (1923). "Martin Tabert of North Dakota." In J. Davis (Ed.) (2002), *The wide brim: Early poems and ponderings of Marjory Stoneman Douglas*. Gainesville, FL: University Press of Florida, pp. 136–137.
18. Douglas, M. (1925). "A Bird Dog in the Hand." *The Saturday Evening Post*. September 12: pp. 6–7, 56, 58, 60, 62.
19. Douglas, M. (1931). "Wings." *The Saturday Evening Post*. March 14: pp. 10–11, 74, 77–78.
20. Douglas, M. (1935). "September-Remember." *The Saturday Evening Post*. December 7: pp. 12–13, 39–40, 42, 46.
21. Douglas, M. (1941). "The Road to the Horizon." *The Saturday Evening Post*. February 22: pp. 14–15, 60, 62–63, 67.
22. Douglas, M. (with J. Rothchild) (1987), p. 180.
23. ibid. p. 233.
24. ibid. p. 189.
25. Allen, H. (1933). *Anthony Adverse*. New York, NY: Rinehart.
26. Douglas, M. (1947), pp. 5–6.

27. ibid. p. 385.

28. Douglas, M. (1952). *Road to the Sun*. New York, NY: Rinehart.

29. Douglas, M. (1953). *Freedom River Florida 1845*. New York, NY: Scribner's.

30. Douglas, M. (1959). *Alligator crossing*. New York, NY: John Day Company.

31. Douglas, M. (1958). *Hurricane*. New York, NY: Rinehart.

32. Douglas, M. (1967). *Florida the long frontier*. New York, NY: Harper & Row.

33. Douglas, M. (1973). *Adventures in a green world–the story of David Fairchild and Barbour Lathrop*. Coconut Grove, FL: Field Research Projects.

34. Douglas, M. (with J. Rothchild) (1987), p. 211.

35. ibid. p. 225.

36. ibid. p. 14.

37. ibid. p. 227.

38. ibid. p. 20

39. ibid.

40. Clinton, W. (1993). "Remarks on presenting the Presidential Medals of Freedom." *Weekly Compilation of Presidential Documents*. 29, 48 (December 6) 2479.

41. Douglas, M. (with J. Rothchild) (1987), p. 166.

42. Davis, J. (2003). "'Conservation is now a Dead Word': Marjory Stoneman Douglas and the Transformation of American Environmentalism." *Environmental History*. Vol. 8, No. 1, pp. 53–76.

43. Nash, R. (1989). *The rights of nature: A history of environmental ethics*. Madison, WI: The University of Wisconsin Press.

44. Leopold, A. (1949). *A sand county almanac*. New York, NY: Oxford University Press.

45. Carson, R. (1962). *Silent spring*. Boston, MA: Houghton Mifflin.

46. Douglas, M. (with J. Rothchild) (1987), p. 232.

47. (no author given) (1983) "Sunday Q & A." *Insights, The Orlando Sentinel*. April 17: pp. 1–2G.

48. Douglas, M. (with J. Rothchild) (1987), p. 23.

49. ibid. p. 250.

VI: Democracy Is a Verb

1. Fuller, R., Agel, I., and Fiore, Q. (1970). *I seem to be a verb*. New York, NY: Bantam Books.

2. Nisbett, R. (2003). *The geography of thought: How Asians and Westerners think differently—and why*. New York, NY: Free Press.

3. McCullough, D. (1995). From a speech given by McCullough upon receiving the "Distinguished Contribution to American Letters Award" at the National Book Awards dinner.

4. ibid.

5. Nash, R. and Graves, G. (1995). *From these beginnings: A biographical approach to American history. Volume 1. Fifth Edition.* New York, NY: Harper Collins.

6. Reiser, O. (1966). *Cosmic humanism.* Cambridge, MA: Schenkman Publishing Company.

7. Leopold, A. (1949). *A sand county almanac.* London, England: Oxford University Press.

8. Gardner, H., Csikszentmihalyi, M. and Damon, W. (2001). *Good work.* New York, NY: Basic Books.

9. ibid. p. xi.

10. Federman, D. (2007). A boy who makes a difference. *Christian Science Monitor,* January, 2.

11. Gardner et al. p. 243.

VII: Afterword: Why We Chose Frederick Law Olmsted, Jane Addams, Benton MacKaye, and Marjory Stoneman Douglas

Frederick Law Olmsted: Doug Wellman

1. Wellman, J. (1987). *Wildland recreation policy: An introduction.* New York, NY: John Wiley.

2. Sax, J. (1980). *Mountains without handrails: Reflections on the national parks.* Ann Arbor, MI: The University of Michigan Press.

3. Roper, L. (1973). *FLO: A biography of Frederick Law Olmsted.* Baltimore, MD: Johns Hopkins University Press.

4. Rbyczysnki, W. (1999). *A clearing in the distance: Frederick Law Olmsted and America in the nineteenth century.* New York, NY: Scribner.

5. Wellman, J., and Tipple, T. (1990). Public forestry and direct democracy. *The Environmental Professional, 12:* 77–86.

Jane Addams: Karla Henderson

1. Hudson, S. (1982). Who was our mother? *Leisure commentary and practice*. Denton, TX: North Texas State University.

2. Henderson, K. (1982). Jane Addams: Pioneer in leisure services. *Journal of Physical Education, Recreation, and Dance, 53*(2): 42–46.

3. Henderson, K. (1992). Invisible pioneers? The impact of women in the recreation movement. *Leisure Sciences, 14:*139–153.

Benton MacKaye: Roger Moore

1. MacKaye, B. (1921, October). An Appalachian Trail: A Project in Regional Planning. *Journal of the American Institute of Architects:* 325–330.

Marjory Stoneman Douglas: Dan Dustin

1. This comment was made by the late Dr. David Gray and former Vice President of California State University at Long Beach, in an education session titled "Publish Don't Perish" at the 1977 National Recreation and Park Association Congress in Las Vegas, Nevada.

About the Authors

Doug Wellman is Professor Emeritus in the College of Natural Resources at North Carolina State University (NCSU) in Raleigh. Dan Dustin is Professor and Chair of the Department of Parks, Recreation, and Tourism in the College of Health at the University of Utah in Salt Lake City. Karla Henderson and Roger Moore are Professor and Associate Professor, respectively, in NCSU's Department of Parks, Recreation, and Tourism Management.

Other Books by Venture Publishing, Inc.

21st Century Leisure: Current Issues, Second Edition
    by Valeria J. Freysinger and John R. Kelly

A•B•Cs of Behavior Change: Skills for Working With Behavior Problems in Nursing Homes
    by Margaret D. Cohn, Michael A. Smyer, and Ann L. Horgas

Activity Experiences and Programming within Long-Term Care
    by Ted Tedrick and Elaine R. Green

The Activity Gourmet
    by Peggy Powers

Adventure Programming
    edited by John C. Miles and Simon Priest

Assessment: The Cornerstone of Activity Programs
    by Ruth Perschbacher

Behavior Modification in Therapeutic Recreation: An Introductory Manual
    by John Datillo and William D. Murphy

Benefits of Leisure
    edited by B.L. Driver, Perry J. Brown, and George L. Peterson

Beyond Baskets and Beads: Activities for Older Adults with Functional Impairments
    by Mary Hart, Karen Primm, and Kathy Cranisky

Beyond Bingo: Innovative Programs for the New Senior
    by Sal Arrigo, Jr., Ann Lewis, and Hank Mattimore

Beyond Bingo 2: More Innovative Programs for the New Senior
    by Sal Arrigo, Jr.

Boredom Busters: Themed Special Events to Dazzle and Delight Your Group
    by Annette C. Moore

Both Gains and Gaps: Feminist Perspectives on Women's Leisure
    by Karla Henderson, M. Deborah Bialeschki, Susan M. Shaw, and Valeria J. Freysinger

Brain Fitness
    by Suzanne Fitzsimmons

Client Assessment in Therapeutic Recreation Services
    by Norma J. Stumbo

Client Outcomes in Therapeutic Recreation Services
    by Norma J. Stumbo

Conceptual Foundations for Therapeutic Recreation
    edited by David R. Austin, John Datillo, and Bryan P. McCormick

Constraints to Leisure
    edited by Edgar L. Jackson

Dementia Care Programming: An Identity-Focused Approach
    by Rosemary Dunne

Dimensions of Choice: Qualitative Approaches to Parks, Recreation, Tourism, Sport, and Leisure Research, Second Edition
by Karla A. Henderson

Diversity and the Recreation Profession: Organizational Perspectives, Revised Edition
edited by Maria T. Allison and Ingrid E. Schneider

Effective Management in Therapeutic Recreation Service, Second Edition
by Marcia Jean Carter and Gerald S. O'Morrow

Evaluating Leisure Services: Making Enlightened Decisions, Second Edition
by Karla A. Henderson and M. Deborah Bialeschki

Everything from A to Y: The Zest Is up to You! Older Adult Activities for Every Day of the Year
by Nancy R. Cheshire and Martha L. Kenney

The Evolution of Leisure: Historical and Philosophical Perspectives
by Thomas Goodale and Geoffrey Godbey

Experience Marketing: Strategies for the New Millennium
by Ellen L. O'Sullivan and Kathy J. Spangler

Facilitation Techniques in Therapeutic Recreation
by John Dattilo

File o' Fun: A Recreation Planner for Games & Activities, Third Edition
by Jane Harris Ericson and Diane Ruth Albright

The Game and Play Leader's Handbook: Facilitating Fun and Positive Interaction, Revised Edition
by Bill Michaelis and John M. O'Connell

The Game Finder—A Leader's Guide to Great Activities
by Annette C. Moore

Getting People Involved in Life and Activities: Effective Motivating Techniques
by Jeanne Adams

Glossary of Recreation Therapy and Occupational Therapy
by David R. Austin

Great Special Events and Activities
by Annie Morton, Angie Prosser, and Sue Spangler

Group Games & Activity Leadership
by Kenneth J. Bulik

Growing With Care: Using Greenery, Gardens, and Nature With Aging and Special Populations
by Betsy Kreidler

Hands On! Children's Activities for Fairs, Festivals, and Special Events
by Karen L. Ramey

Health Promotion for Mind, Body and Spirit
by Suzanne Fitzsimmons and Linda L. Buettner

In Search of the Starfish: Creating a Caring Environment
by Mary Hart, Karen Primm, and Kathy Cranisky

Inclusion: Including People With Disabilities in Parks and Recreation Opportunities
by Lynn Anderson and Carla Brown Kress

Inclusive Leisure Services: Responding to the Rights of People with Disabilities, Second Edition
    by John Dattilo
Innovations: A Recreation Therapy Approach to Restorative Programs
    by Dawn R. De Vries and Julie M. Lake
Internships in Recreation and Leisure Services: A Practical Guide for Students, Fourth Edition
    by Edward E. Seagle, Jr. and Ralph W. Smith
Interpretation of Cultural and Natural Resources, Second Edition
    by Douglas M. Knudson, Ted T. Cable, and Larry Beck
Intervention Activities for At-Risk Youth
    by Norma J. Stumbo
Introduction to Outdoor Recreation: Providing and Managing Resource Based Opportunities
    by Roger L. Moore and B.L. Driver
Introduction to Recreation and Leisure Services, Eighth Edition
    by Karla A. Henderson, M. Deborah Bialeschki, John L. Hemingway, Jan S. Hodges,
        Beth D. Kivel, and H. Douglas Sessoms
Introduction to Therapeutic Recreation: U.S. and Canadian Perspectives
    by Kenneth Mobily and Lisa Ostiguy
*Introduction to Writing Goals and Objectives: A Manual for Recreation Therapy Students
        and Entry-Level Professionals*
    by Suzanne Melcher
Leadership and Administration of Outdoor Pursuits, Third Edition
    by James Blanchard, Michael Strong, and Phyllis Ford
Leadership in Leisure Services: Making a Difference, Third Edition
    by Debra J. Jordan
Leisure and Leisure Services in the 21st Century: Toward Mid Century
    by Geoffrey Godbey
Leisure Education I: A Manual of Activities and Resources, Second Edition
    by Norma J. Stumbo
Leisure Education II: More Activities and Resources, Second Edition
    by Norma J. Stumbo
Leisure Education III: More Goal-Oriented Activities
    by Norma J. Stumbo
Leisure Education IV: Activities for Individuals with Substance Addictions
    by Norma J. Stumbo
Leisure Education Program Planning: A Systematic Approach, Third Edition
    by John Dattilo
Leisure for Canadians
    edited by Ron McCarville and Kelly MacKay
Leisure Education Specific Programs
    by John Dattilo
Leisure Studies: Prospects for the Twenty-First Century
    edited by Edgar L. Jackson and Thomas L. Burton

Therapeutic Activity Intervention with the Elderly: Foundations and Practices
    by Barbara A. Hawkins, Marti E. May, and Nancy Brattain Rogers
Therapeutic Recreation and the Nature of Disabilities
    by Kenneth E. Mobily and Richard D. MacNeil
Therapeutic Recreation: Cases and Exercises, Second Edition
    by Barbara C. Wilhite and M. Jean Keller
Therapeutic Recreation in Health Promotion and Rehabilitation
    by John Shank and Catherine Coyle
Therapeutic Recreation in the Nursing Home
    by Linda Buettner and Shelley L. Martin
Therapeutic Recreation Programming: Theory and Practice
    by Charles Sylvester, Judith E. Voelkl, and Gary D. Ellis
Therapeutic Recreation Protocol for Treatment of Substance Addictions
    by Rozanne W. Faulkner
The Therapeutic Recreation Stress Management Primer
    by Cynthia Mascott
The Therapeutic Value of Creative Writing
    by Paul M. Spicer
Tourism and Society: A Guide to Problems and Issues
    by Robert W. Wyllie
Traditions: Improving Quality of Life in Caregiving
    by Janelle Sellick
Trivia by the Dozen: Encouraging Interaction and Reminiscence in Managed Care
    by Jean Vetter

Venture Publishing, Inc.
1999 Cato AvenueState College, PA 16801
Phone: 814-234-4561
Fax: 814-234-1651